ADVANCE PRAISE

"In *The Antifragility Edge*, Alhir provides practical advice and guidance for those seeking to build and nurture an organization that is fit for the challenges we face in today's world as well as being fit for the future. Proven through his impressive work in the trenches, readers are sure to benefit from an artfully crafted approach that is always context sensitive and places the human aspects of an enterprise front and center."
Brad Barton, Coach & Consultant and co-author of *Conscious Agility: Conscious Capitalism + Business Agility = Antifragility*

"There is a massive and urgent need for developing practical literature and a dialog on the application of Nassim Taleb's seminal concept of antifragility. Our beliefs and world infrastructure reflect inherent fragility that not only limits our comprehension, it endangers our society. Si Alhir has contributed significantly to the emerging field of antifragility, and in *The Antifragility Edge* he explores how antifragility may be operationalized by individuals and organizations to achieve greater antifragility."
Tony Bendell, Organisational Consultant and author of *Building Anti-Fragile Organisations: Risk, Opportunity and Governance in a Turbulent World*

"Sinan Si Alhir offers a way for organisations to feed on disruption. He offers strategies for flourishing in chaos, embracing today's global economic uncertainties. This is strategic thinking for a new world – one in which so much of what you thought you could rely on no longer applies."
David Cushman, Business Consultant and author of *The 10 Principles of Open Business: Building Success in Today's Open Economy*

"What's next? That is a question that I have heard countless times over the past few years. Si Alhir answers that question, providing a guide that will help individuals, teams, and organizations become more resilient and future-proof (antifragile) than most could even imagine. Si's unique perspective, vast experience and practical knowledge, and sheer pragmatism all come together to give the reader of *The Antifragility Edge* a pathway to the future. If you want to change your paradigm and thrive in an environment of volatility, uncertainty, complexity, and ambiguity (VUCA), this is a must read."
Steve Fastabend, Organizational Transformation Coach

"Si has always demonstrated the ability to keenly appreciate and artfully blend, integrate, and put into practice the crucial concepts across a vast assortment of bodies of experience to help individuals, teams, and enterprises transform to a healthier place and achieve their business goals. *The Antifragility Edge* advances this art to a whole new level beyond integrating these foundational concepts, but offers a more holistic approach to actualize results. If you take the time to deeply digest this integrated work and all the guidance it offers, you will be equipped to profoundly shift your enterprise to a place where it can thrive in an increasingly turbulent marketplace."

Mark Ferraro, Coach & Consultant and
co-author of *Conscious Agility: Conscious Capitalism*
+ Business Agility = Antifragility

"Alhir has taken the world-changing ideas of Nassim Taleb and translated them into practical advice that an executive or organization development practitioner can make use of. His depth of understanding of both worlds – antifragility and organizational development – is evident and *The Antifragility Edge* is a must-read for the informed practitioner."

Paul Gibbons, Consultant and author of
The Science of Successful Organizational Change: How Leaders Set Strategy, Change Behavior, and Create an Agile Culture

"Sinan Si Alhir has made a great contribution to understating the individual and collective areas of antifragility, resilience, growth, change and organizational design. And he has done it in a style that is both a practitioner's style and a conceptual synthesizer. Usually one gets one or the other. Indeed, the great merit of the book is the building of bridges between different angles and approaches, all of them seeing life through their particular glasses. Si seems to sit at the summit of the conceptual mountain and let all those approaches climb up, and convene at a level that can facilitate the conversation. As such, the conversation launches more questions than provides answers. Taleb's brain is probably made of different substance than most of us mortals, but he is not an organizational practitioner. The bridges between antifragile land and other lands are still in construction. One at least is now built enough to walk in. And this is Si's book."
Dr. Leandro Herrero, Chief Organization Architect, The Chalfont Project, and pioneer of The Viral Change Mobilizing Platform

"In his latest book, Si Alhir has transformed antifragility from being a mostly academic and abstract concept and applied it to the real world that you and I experience every day. Alhir demonstrates and shows, in all clarity and simplicity, how antifragility can come alive in individuals, in organizations, in businesses, in everything, really, if we understand how to apply it. It is a book not just about how to run your business, in the end it is also about how to run your life, successfully."
Jan Husdal, Resilience Adviser

"Si Alhir has done fundamental work in illustrating the challenges we – as individuals, managers, citizens and community members – are facing when entering the Postnormal VUCA Era. He not only takes Nassim Nicholas Taleb's brilliant theories to the more practical level but he also gives extremely valuable food for thought on how to improve our 'vucability' level. Si's masterpiece is highly recommended reading for those who want to thrive also in the emergent Postnormal Era."

Ilkka Kakko, Founder and Partner in Karostech Ltd. and author of *Oasis Way and the Postnormal Era – How Understanding Serendipity Will Lead You to Success*

"Precise, concise, penetrating, and illuminating, *The Antifragility Edge* is the perfect companion to Nassim Nicholas Taleb's masterwork, *Antifragile*. Effectively balancing out the often evocative bombast of Taleb's didactic style with a clean, objective, and dispassionate discourse, Alhir's approach is the balance needed for the professional reader who desires something to augment, deepen, and smooth out Taleb's brilliant and enjoyable but sometimes overwhelming displays of self-serving emotion. If you love Taleb, and who doesn't, Alhir offers the perfect 'workbook' for the consultant, coach, or knowledgeable or lay reader. If Taleb has written the bible on Antifragility, a distinction that he coined, then Alhir's intelligent and highly accessible book, *The Antifragility Edge* is a must read for the practitioner."

John King, Cultural Architect and co-author of *Tribal Leadership: Leveraging Natural Groups to Build a Thriving Organization*

"Si Alhir wields a sharp antifragility edge as he slices through the OODA loop to free up new strategies for dealing with volatility, uncertainty, complexity and uncertainty (otherwise known as VUCA). His practical field guide to antifragility will help organizations at every level: individual, collective and enterprise. Given the reality of exponential change, this book is a timely addition to every business leader's library."

Doug Kirkpatrick, Organizational Consultant and author of *Beyond Empowerment: The Age of the Self-Managed Organization*

"Nearly every organization is asking the same question today: How to survive in the fast-paced, unpredictable competitive environment into which we are accelerating? Alhir offers an answer to an even more exciting possibility: How can organizations redesign themselves to thrive because of the historic shift in the pace of competition? By applying some of the practical advice Alhir outlines in *The Antifragility Edge*, we can turn volatility, uncertainty, complexity, and ambiguity into allies."

Kaihan Krippendorff, Founder of Outthinker and author of *Outthink the Competition: How a New Generation of Strategists Sees Options Others Ignore*; *The Way of Innovation: Master the Five Elements of Change to Reinvent Your Products, Services, and Organization*; *Hide a Dagger Behind a Smile: Use the 36 Ancient Chinese Strategies to Seize the Competitive Edge*; and *The Art of the Advantage: 36 Strategies to Seize the Competitive Edge*

"Si Alhir – with combination of first-hand practical experience, deep heartfelt sincerity, and sharp intellect – has written the book to future-proof (antifragility) you, your business, and your teams. Si takes abstract concepts and translates them into very human applications that not only changes the way you look at business, but changes the way you look at life."
James Key Lim, Entrepreneur, Business Consultant, and former CEO of Zappos Delivering Happiness at Work based upon #1 NYT best seller by Tony Hsieh, CEO of Zappos.com

"Much has been written and discussed around the need for business agility in times of constant change. But what if you could not only react quickly, but indeed thrive among the chaos, benefitting from it and using the sudden changes and shifting needs to your advantage? To enable that superpower, one must be antifragile, the opposite of fragility, reenergizing from change instead of crumbling under it. Think of what that could do for decision-making and planning in times of great uncertainty, volatility, and unpredictable change events – innovating, experimenting, and coming out ahead while others are merely trying to survive. That is what Si Alhir's insightful book offers, illuminating and building upon Nassim Nicholas Taleb's original antifragility concept in great clarity and simplicity, and with an action plan that can be put to use immediately. Indeed, it will infuse you and your organization with an adventurous and entrepreneurial spirit that will take you beyond adaptability to true innovation. It's an indispensable tool for any change leadership toolkit."
Jerry Manas, Consultant and author of *Managing the Gray Areas: Essential Insights for Leading People, Projects & Organizations*

"In an age of random and non-linear opportunity, Sinan Si Alhir has written an important, urgent book. Packed with indispensable insights, it will help future leaders raise their game."
Anne McCrossan, founder of Visceral Business

"Sinan Si Alhir understands that fragility can be detected, measured, and transformed despite crisis, collapse, and transition. His new book provides badass, practical, and actionable guidance for achieving antifragility. Insight and innovation comes from the fringe, 'the edge'. In the words of Sinan Si Alhir, 'antifragility is a delicate dance – at the antifragility edge – between reality and aliveness.'"
Kirsten Osolind, Managing Partner and SVP of Strategy and Innovation with RE:INVENTION Consulting

"Understanding systems and domino effects is essential in this era of complexity. That is why a voice such as Sinan Si Alhir is so important. He takes an eagle's view of the landscape and is able to extract what is essential. He then has the gift of the aesthetic to bring information to scale in a way that is not only accessible but is also beautiful. That is exactly what he has done here in *The Antifragility Edge*. As a reader you will make new connections. As a leader you will better understand cause/effect. As an individual you will have more discernment."
Jennifer Sertl, Business Strategist and co-author of *Strategy, Leadership and the Soul: Resilience, Responsiveness and Reflection for a Global Economy*

"Si Alhir explores the phenomenon, impacts and implications of antifragility in this work, and he uniquely does so at the individual, collective and enterprise levels. Si is a foremost expert on the topic of antifragility. Leaders and would-be leaders of all organizations seeking to not only survive, but thrive, in an era of unpredictability and rapid global change are advised to study and become antifragile. In *The Antifragility Edge: Antifragility in Practice*, Si proves an expert guide and practitioner. He makes the difficult concepts and theories behind antifragility eminently practical and meaningful – at the individual, group, and corporate levels. This work will empower you to embrace disruption and change while the competition is struggling to orient and respond."

Becky Sheetz, Speaker & Trainer and author of *The Art of War for Small Business* and *Sun Tzu for Women*

"Most people fear the inevitable uncertainty of our complex modern world. However, Si Alhir explains in *The Antifragility Edge* how we can benefit from leveraging the unpredictability and lead ourselves, our teams and organizations towards better futures. His ideas enable us to discover options and opportunities that we could not have imagined with traditional thinking and approaches."

Dr. Arthur Shelley, author of
The Organizational Zoo, Being a Successful Knowledge Leader, and *KNOWledge SUCCESSion*

"Change creates disorder and the systems we put in place to manage change create even more disorder. Sinan Si Alhir does an admirable job of helping the reader to think through their own systematic approach to change-management so that we can all better design solutions to problems that are not just robust, they are antifragile!"
Lex Sisney, author of *Organizational Physics - The Science of Growing a Business*

"Sinan Si Alhir has taken the most powerful current thinking about resilience, adaptation, and organizational transformation and synthesized it in a brand new way. Antifragility is absolutely necessary for thriving during rapid, sometimes unceasing and extraordinary change, and can give organizations a powerful edge."
Karlin Sloan, CEO of Sloan Group International

"Leaders know the goal is to thrive (not just survive) in our VUCA world, and inspire their teams and organizations to do so as well. Alhir offers a wealth of actionable insights to equip leaders to do just that, emerging stronger and better than before, individually and collectively."
Barbara Trautlein, Principal of Change Catalysts, LLC and author of *Change Intelligence: Use the Power of CQ to Lead Change that Sticks*

SINAN SI ALHIR

THE ANTI-FRAGILITY EDGE

ANTIFRAGILITY IN PRACTICE

Published by
LID Publishing Inc.
31 West 34th Street, 8th Floor, Suite 8004,
New York, NY 10001, US

One Adam Street, London WC2N 6LE

info@lidpublishing.com
www.lidpublishing.com
A member of:

BPR
Business Publishers Roundtable

www.businesspublishersroundtable.com

Printed in the United States
ISBN: 978-0-9969433-0-7

Cover and page design: Caroline Li

SINAN SI ALHIR

THE ANTI-FRAGILITY EDGE

ANTIFRAGILITY IN PRACTICE

LONDON   NEW YORK   SHANGHAI
MADRID   BARCELONA   BOGOTA
MEXICO CITY   MONTERREY   BUENOS AIRES

DEDICATION

To my father Saad, mother Rabab,
wife Milad, and daughter Nora.
Thank you for enduring me.

CONTENTS

ACKNOWLE

DGEMENTS

Why antifragility?

With the soul of a practitioner, my consulting and coaching practice is rooted in Sun Tzu's *Art of War* and working with chaos, which is inherent to reality. Fundamentally, I partner with clients and work with chaos in advancing their flourishing.

Nassim Nicholas Taleb's *Antifragile: Things that Gain from Disorder* (2012) crystalizes that antifragility is about disorder and growth (or gain). Given that disorder and chaos are near synonymous and given that growth and flourishing are near synonymous, among other reasons, the congruence and synergy of antifragility with my consulting and coaching was almost intuitive. Given that flourishing involves being alive and thriving in reality, and given that partnering involves a 'delicate dance' of integrating disparate aspects, partnering with clients and working with chaos in advancing their flourishing is a journey that is always 'delicate' and always at the 'edge' of success and failure, a delicate dance between reality and aliveness.

Perhaps what resonates most about antifragility, with me, is what resonates most about Sun Tzu's *Art of War*, its 'naturalness'.

Why mindsets, questions, leadership, conversations, relationships, behaviours, groups, dysfunctions, conflict, teaming, communities, adaptive cycles, and panarchy?

Again, with the soul of a practitioner, these aspects were 'revealed through practice' and 'born from practice' to form the skeleton of this book. They fundamentally reify our human nature and human dynamics in the context of the human condition.

There are a number of individuals who made this book possible, specifically those who endured me – the 'bundle of chaos' that I am or the 'epitome of chaos' as some have proclaimed I am.

My father Saad and mother Rabab, thank you for giving me life and nurturing me throughout the journey of life. My wife Milad and daughter Nora, thank you for enduring me throughout the journey. My family members, thank you for sharing in the journey. My mentor, Carl V. Page, the father of Larry Page (co-founder of Google), thank you for remaining present on the journey.

My wife Milad, thank you for being you and thank you for embracing who I am.

My daughter Nora, thank you for forcing me to learn those things that I failed to learn throughout my life and forcing me to unlearn some things that I learned throughout my life.

Nassim Nicholas Taleb, the 'father of Antifragility' and the 'father of Black Swans', thank you for raising our awareness of black swans and antifragility.

Carol Dweck, Marilee G. Adams, Barbara A. Trautlein, Judith E. Glaser, Dave Logan, John King, Halee Fischer-Wright, Leandro Herrero, Bruce Wayne Tuckman, Patrick Lencioni, Kenneth W. Thomas, Ralph H. Kilmann, Amy C. Edmondson, Étienne Wenger, and Crawford Stanley Holling, thank you for your wisdom. While your wisdom has proven to be demonstrably beneficial in fostering antifragility in practice, as entrepreneurs and adventurers, we'll respectfully continuously and endlessly leverage stress to discover even more wisdom for fostering antifragility.

Judith E. Glaser, thank you for your wisdom and thank you for contributing the Forward to this book. You and your wisdom are a 'gift' to the world. You are deeply appreciated.

Brad Barton, Tony Bendell, David Cushman, Steve Fastabend, Mark Ferraro, Paul Gibbons, Leandro Herrero, Jan Husdal, Ilkka Kakko, John King, Doug Kirkpatrick, Kaihan Krippendorff, James Key Lim, Jerry Manas, Anne McCrossan, Kirsten Osolind, Jennifer Sertl, Becky Sheetz, Arthur Shelley, Lex Sisney, Karlin Sloan, and Barbara Trautlein, thank you for your thoughts and contributing advance praise for this book. You and your comments mean more than you know. You are deeply appreciated.

Brad Barton, Mark Ferraro, and Steve Fastabend, thank you for your partnership over the years. We are indeed students of human nature and human dynamics in the context of the human condition. Looking forward to continuing to explore the notion that the human animal, with its human nature, is the most dangerous animal in its natural habitat.

Sara Taheri, Andrew Mueller, and Martin Liu of LID Publishing, thank you for your patience, believing in this book, and everything you contributed to make this book real. And others with LID Publishing, thank you for everything you contributed to make this book real.

I would also like to thank all of my clients and colleagues – both those who have partnered with me and those who have seemingly not partnered with me over the years – for the stress that has energized me to adapt and survive as well as evolve and thrive. Thank you for allowing me to foster your antifragility and thank you for fostering my antifragility.

I will not forget any of you, and I only ask that you please remember me.

FORWARD BY

JUDITH E. GLASER

Si and I met about a decade ago. I had no way of putting words to his brilliance and insatiable curiosity. He had an appetite for learning – and it went further than that. He had an unbridled spirit to learn and to know more and do more with what he was learning than almost anyone I had ever met.

He wasn't satisfied with learning what others knew. He was gifted with the desire and ability to learn something new, integrate it with other concepts, and transform his perspectives into new ways that could bring wisdom and insight to others. That framework for facing reality with gusto and curiosity has enabled Si to embrace and also add to our understanding of Antifragility, introduced by Nassim Nicholas Taleb in *Antifragile: Things That Gain from Disorder* – a new concept that helps us think about and understand the new DNA for the 21st Century.

Behind this new word are concepts that Si brings to life – as he paints a world that is evolving around us; a vision that asks us to embrace rather than fear our world of constant changes; a world that calls us to work **with others** rather than **against others**; and a world that beckons us to see 'shocks' as activators of our next level of greatness, and toughness. With this comes a new wisdom for taking on and understanding that change will not recede – instead will become what defines success.

WHAT CREATES GROWTH?

One of the most powerful and important aspects of our human growth system is the ability to overcome adversity. When our adversity is adversaries, we can use strategies for defending ourselves such as attacking back when adversaries come after us, we can run away and protect ourselves, and we can give in to what is happening in order to quell the fire, so to speak. These are self-defence options that have been transferred from generation to generation – and represent I-centric thinking.

We are, however, in a new epic time in our history where **changes** drive us every day, 24/7. We have no choice; we cannot stop changes from taking place. We have become a highly interactive, highly engaging world, and engagements and interaction creates conflicts, disruptions and in the best of all worlds – disruptive innovations – and that's a good thing. Healthy engagement extends our life span. When we become isolated, and fail to engage, we shorten our life span – this is part of the Neuroscience of WE® (http://www.creatingwe.com/institute/about-the-institute/33-keynotes/235-neuroscience-of-we). Human beings need each other to grow and shared 'growth challenges' activate a higher performing immune system that extends our lives, gives us new strengths for tackling difficult challenges and prevents us from stepping back from the changes that bring us our greatest success.

SO WHERE DOES ALL THIS FIT INTO THIS WONDERFUL BOOK, *THE ANTIFRAGILITY EDGE?*

Si nailed it when he identified that what human beings need to thrive, is to redefine how we think and act around the changes and challenges of our lives. To think of challenges and changes as something healthy – **something that is built into our immune systems as a requirement for activating our immune systems for growth, and something that happens through our conversations with others.** So in this incredible book you will discover how to become a 'change Ninja', and learn how to arrest the fear we have built up for 'being shocked by lightning of change' and see this as a new channel for growth.

CONVERSATIONAL EPIGENETICS

Conversations activate growth and strength – if we know that we can create more space in our lives for the kind of conversations that bring insight and healthy change – we need to make more space for this. Our Creating WE Institute has spent decades in researching companies comparing those that are enormously successful to those that are not. In Si's new book we see many powerful ways to get in front of the change curve and catalyze growth in our teams, our organizations and ourselves.

We've learned from the field of Epigenetics that 50% of our DNA has been encoded to be activated by the environment, and 50% has been encoded to be impervious to change or impact. This means – translated into everyday language – that conversations between and among people are the most powerful environment that activates change. So as you read this book, keep in mind that a new framework is emerging in the world. One that asks us to catalyze new thinking, to challenge each other – to even 'shock' each other into experimenting, testing out and partnering for success.

Judith E. Glaser is CEO of Benchmark Communications, Inc. and Chairman of The Creating WE Institute. She is an Organizational Anthropologist, and consults to Fortune 500 Companies. Judith is the author of *Conversational Intelligence: How Great Leaders Build Trust and Get Extraordinary Results* (Bibliomotion). Visit www.conversationalintelligence.com; jeglaser@ creatingwe.com, 212-307-4386

INTROD

UCTION

Today, business organizations experience unprecedented levels of disruption (turbulence) and can only expect the unexpected. While they must perform in a world characterized by volatility, uncertainty, complexity, and ambiguity (VUCA), their ability to observe, orient, decide, and act (OODA) is no longer enough to survive and thrive amid disorder. In this new chaotic reality, while agility is essential for adapting and surviving, antifragility is essential for evolving and thriving. Business organizations must embrace this new reality and emerge stronger.

ANTIFRAGILITY

In *Antifragile: Things that Gain from Disorder* (2012), Nassim Nicholas Taleb introduces antifragility.

Some things benefit from shocks; they thrive and grow when exposed to volatility, randomness, disorder, and stressors and love adventure, risk, and uncertainty. Yet, in spite of the ubiquity of the phenomenon, there is no word for the exact opposite of fragile. Let us call it antifragile.

First, Taleb distinguishes between the fragile, robust, and antifragile (the 'triad'):

The fragile wants tranquillity, the antifragile grows from disorder, and the robust doesn't care too much.

Next, Taleb advances that:

By grasping the mechanisms of antifragility we can build a systematic and broad guide to non-predictive decision-making under uncertainty in business, politics, medicine, and life in general.

As the world becomes increasingly interconnected and interdependent, 'black swans' – large-scale, unpredictable, and irregular events of massive consequence – are inevitably becoming more prominent. It is far more reasonable to figure out whether something is fragile than to calculate the risks and probabilities of rare events that may harm it.

As a result of the proliferation of VUCA, non-predictive decision-making while using OODA in simple or obvious, complicated, complex, and chaotic environments (the Cynefin framework) is essential. For business organizations to embrace this new chaotic reality and emerge stronger, they must embody an antifragility edge.

In *The Antifragility Edge: Antifragility in Practice*, I will demystify antifragility, explore how antifragility may be operationalized or put into practice by business organizations (at the individual, collective, and enterprise levels), and offer an actionable roadmap for how business organizations can achieve greater antifragility and adapt, survive, evolve, and thrive in a chaotic world. We'll explore various insights through practical examples. You'll be able to immediately start using these practical ideas to embrace reality and emerge stronger.

COACHING FOR ANTIFRAGILITY

As a consultant and coach, I am a catalyst or alchemist – a student of human nature and human dynamics in the context of the human condition. I foster success by partnering with clients in advancing their business outcomes and by aligning and bridging intentions and impacts that are valued by my clients' clients and customers. I have often explored the notion that the human animal, with its human nature, is the most dangerous animal in its natural habitat. Perhaps what resonates most about antifragility (and chaos and disorder and disruption), with me, is its 'naturalness'.

I appreciate the definition of coaching by the International Coach Federation (ICF) (2016):

Coaching is partnering with clients in a thought-provoking and creative process that inspires them to maximize their personal and professional potential.

And I appreciate Tom Landry's (2016) articulation of a coach:

A coach is someone who tells you what you don't want to hear, who has you see what you don't want to see, so you can be who you have always known you could be.

Fundamentally, I partner with individuals, collectives of individuals, and enterprises of individuals and collectives to curiously and creatively provoke (using micro-coaching interventions, moments, and events) an experience that fosters awareness so that the participants' true nature emerges and so that potential is actualized. To coach is to curiously and creatively provoke, to nudge, or to stress within a specific context. And always, before I engage in a coaching relationship, I seek permission from the individual, collective, or enterprise that I am coaching.

In *The Antifragility Edge: Antifragility in Practice*, I focus on providing foundational background information to the various topics that foster antifragility and also provide practical examples and insights, from my consulting and coaching practice, that will help you to achieve greater antifragility.

With the soul of a practitioner, I put foundational information into practice and I refine that knowledge based on practice, continuously and endlessly fostering success in partnership with others. As a coach, my approach herein involves asking many questions to curiously and creatively provoke you.

Please note that I've removed many specifics and details from the examples so as not to reveal personal or professional information, and have focused instead on essential insights. Additionally, I have intentionally repeated some text in various places so that you can read Chapters 2, 3, 4, and 5 in any order after Chapter 1 and you can read almost any chapter section in any order after the chapter introduction.

CHAPTER 1

WHAT IS ANTI-FRAGILITY?

This chapter explores reality; distinguishes between fragility and antifragility; and explores the concept of agility through adapting and surviving, and the concept of antifragility through evolving and thriving.

Consider any thing or entity – an individual, a collective of individuals, or an enterprise (ecosystem) of individuals and collectives in a specific context or environment. For these entities:

- a strength is a positive internal quality or characteristic of an entity that gives or offers it an advantage over other entities
- a weakness is a negative internal quality or characteristic of an entity that places it at a disadvantage relative to other entities
- an opportunity is a positive external situation or factor that an entity could exploit to its advantage
- a threat is a negative external situation or factor that could cause challenges for an entity.

An entity must identify, distinguish between, and respond appropriately to create, discover, develop, and seize opportunities and address threats as well as maximize strengths and minimize weaknesses:

- a strength-opportunity strategy involves an entity aggressively pursuing opportunities that are a good fit for its strengths
- a weakness-opportunity strategy involves an entity overcoming its weaknesses to pursue opportunities
- a strength-threat strategy involves an entity using its strengths to reduce its vulnerability to threats

- a weakness-threat strategy involves an entity defensively preventing its weaknesses from making it susceptible to threats
  - a weakness-strength strategy involves an entity converting its weaknesses into strengths
  - a threat-opportunity strategy involves an entity converting its threats into opportunities.

Reality restricts the interplay between strengths, weaknesses, opportunities, and threats, as an entity interacts with reality and experiences reality to realize its intentions.

For example, consider yourself individually, as a collective of individuals, or as a whole enterprise of individuals and collectives in a specific context or environment. What are the strengths, weaknesses, opportunities, threats, and strategies, for you, each individual, each collective, and the enterprise? What is the interplay between all of these strengths, weaknesses, opportunities, threats, and strategies as individuals, collectives, and the enterprise interact with reality and experience reality to realize their various intentions?

The individual is an 'I', the collective is a 'we', and the enterprise is a holistic 'We' of 'Is' and 'wes'. Every I, we, and We has its own intentions. Anything that requires an I, we, or We to apply its energy to advance and achieve an outcome is a stressor and causes the I, we, and We stress.

REALITY

What is the nature of reality? How do we interact with reality? And how do we experience reality?

Many individuals, collectives, and enterprises experience reality and interact with reality through fear and doubt – sometimes experienced as stress due to the impact of fairness, ownership, reciprocity, cooperation, expression, status, relatedness, autonomy, mastery, stability, certainty, simplicity, clarity, directness, and much more.

It is quite an epiphany to shift or reframe perspectives from fear or doubt to the ideas that reality is volatile, uncertain, complex, and ambiguous; that I, we, and We observe, orient, decide, and act; and that my or our experience of reality is that reality is simple or obvious, complicated, complex, and chaotic.

The Nature of Reality: Volatility, Uncertainty, Complexity, and Ambiguity (VUCA)

What is the nature of reality? Chaos. Paradox. VUCA (2016) (volatility, uncertainty, complexity, and ambiguity) is a military term emphasizing the nature of reality:

Volatility (the V of VUCA) involves the absence of stability. Consider your life: what remains reasonably stable and does not change much throughout your day?

Uncertainty (the U of VUCA) involves the absence of certainty. Consider your life: what can you be reasonably certain will not change much throughout your day?

Complexity (the C of VUCA) involves the absence of simplicity. Consider your life: what is reasonably simple and fully understood throughout your day?

Ambiguity (the A of VUCA) involves the absence of clarity. Consider your life: what is reasonably clear and fully understood throughout your day?

If one extreme (complete disorder) is characterized by VUCA, the other extreme (complete order) is characterized by stability, certainty, simplicity, and clarity (SCSC). Reality lies in between VUCA and SCSC, and we experience reality as turbulent.

Volatility, uncertainty, complexity, and ambiguity present opportunities (or more formally called 'positive risks') and threats (or more formally called 'negative risks') based on strengths and weaknesses. The key is to identify, distinguish between, and respond appropriately to create, discover, develop, and seize opportunities and address threats as well as maximize strengths and minimize weaknesses. VUCA are neither good nor bad; they just are. Again, consider your life and the opportunities and threats that emerge based on your strengths and weaknesses.

Interacting with Reality: Observe, Orient, Decide, and Act (OODA)

How do we interact with reality, given that it is volatile, uncertain, complex, and ambiguous? John Richard Boyd (2016) suggested a four-part cycle (or loop) – OODA – for how we interact with reality.

OBSERVE, ORIENT, DECIDE, AND ACT (OODA)

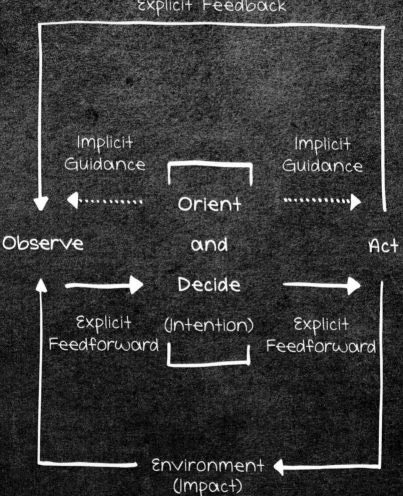

Observation (the first O of OODA) involves sensing or experiencing the environment while being implicitly influenced by our orientation and explicitly influenced by our decisions and actions. Consider what you observe in your environment. Consider how your orientation and decisions influence your observations. Consider how your actions influence your observations. When we fluidly observe and decide, we commonly experience this as intuition.

Orientation (the second O of OODA) involves making sense of our observations. Sense-making involves integrating (or analysing and synthesizing) new information from our observations, previous experience, genetic heritage, and cultural traditions. Consider how you integrate new information, your experience, and history when you try to make sense of reality.

Decision (the D of OODA) involves making decisions while being explicitly influenced by our orientation. Consider how you make decisions based on how you make sense of reality.

Action (the A of OODA) involves enacting or expressing ourselves in the environment while being implicitly influenced by our orientation and explicitly influenced by our decisions. If the environment has changed by the time an action is occurring (since the time of observation, orientation, and decision), there is a mismatch between the action and environment, which is ultimately experienced as disorientation. Consider what actions you enact in your environment. Consider how your orientation and decisions influence your actions. When we fluidly decide and act, we commonly experience this as improvisation.

People commonly use the notions of **purpose** and **meaning** to achieve orientation and to make decisions. What gives people meaning is expressed through their values. What gives people purpose is expressed through their intentions or cause. People orient themselves and make decisions based on their purpose and their values. Orientation is a form of inquiry that integrates an external perspective and an internal perspective.

People commonly use the notion of **outcome** to reference the result of an action that is valued by others and **impact** to reference the ramifications of an action that is valued by others. Therefore, outcomes align and bridge intentions and impacts.

People commonly use the notion of **options** to reference the various ways that they may decide. Our choices are really our options. For example, we can decide to choose option A or option B based on their advantages and disadvantages. Exploring options, making decisions, and taking actions must be done in a timely manner so as to ensure we don't get disorientated.

People commonly use the notion of **experiments** (trial and error, tinkering, or tweaking) to reference the refinement of their orientation based on their decisions, actions, and observations. Our questions are really our experiments. For example, we can refine our orientation based on our decision to choose option A or option B and based on our actions and observations. Performing experiments, making decisions, and taking actions must be done in a timely manner so as to ensure we don't get disorientated.

Additionally, a **plan** may be considered to be a collection of decisions made at a point in time, perhaps about scope, time, and budget or value; internal constraints or reality; or external constraints or reality. A plan allows us to recognize our decisions and our options as things change and to make further decisions as things change. Recognizing a collection of decisions and our options allows us to be more fluid and flow through our circumstances and reality. Furthermore, holistically integrating and balancing everything (content of observations, orientation, decisions, and actions in the context of reality) is crucial. Observe, orient, decide, and act opportunistically.

Orienting and deciding require great awareness of our internal reality (ourselves) and of our identity (who, why, and what). Critical thinking is essential to orienting and deciding, and it involves being aware and self-reflective – asking many questions and being critical of our orientation and decisions as well as of our actions and observations – so as to ensure nothing is missed.

Observing and acting require great awareness of our external reality (where and when). Deliberate practice is essential to observing and acting, which involve being sufficiently aware to question our actions and observations as well as our orientation and decisions, so as to improve them.

Critical thinking and deliberate practice applied at the appropriate level of abstraction, or a reasonable level of detail, for problem solving and the scientific method (trial and error) foster clarity. This is the essence of design. **Empathy** involves appreciating or recognizing – not judging as 'good' or 'bad' – another individual's, collective's, or enterprise's observations, orientation, decisions, and actions based on their perspective. When we so integrate our internal reality and external reality, we commonly experience this as **presence**. Our ability to integrate our internal reality and external reality, and regulate ourselves and our energy, is crucial in enabling us to be more fluid and to flow through our circumstances and reality. We have a type of 'heartbeat' that is our rate of individual fluidity and collective flow through our circumstances and reality.

The OODA loop is not merely a linear sequence of observing, then orienting, then deciding, and then acting; these things must be done continuously and simultaneously, and re-orienting is crucial to interacting with reality. Agility involves changing orientation as well as implicit influence vs. explicit influence, thus being better able to interact with reality. Again, consider your life, the opportunities and threats that exist based on your strengths and weaknesses, and how you are observing, orienting, deciding, and acting.

Experiencing Reality: The Cynefin Framework

Given that reality is volatile, uncertain, complex, and ambiguous and that we interact with reality by observing, orienting, deciding, and acting, how do we experience reality? In a model known as the Cynefin framework, David John Snowden (2007) suggests four domains of how we experience reality: simple or obvious, complicated, complex, and chaotic.

The **obvious domain** involves 'known knowns' (things we know that we know) where we can use best practice to categorize (orient and decide) what we sense (observe) and then respond (act), since cause and effect are evident. This domain is commonly characterized by a sense–categorize–respond pattern. Consider all of the more routine activities you do in your environment; they perhaps require more simple choices.

The **complicated domain** involves 'known unknowns' (things we know that we don't know) where we can use good practice to analyse (orient and decide) what we sense (observe) and then respond (act), since cause and effect are discoverable. This domain is commonly characterized by a sense–analyse–respond pattern. Consider all the activities you do in your environment that require expertise; they perhaps require complicated choices.

The obvious and complicated domains presume an ordered reality – a reality that is more stable, certain, simple, and clear and where the relationship between cause and effect are perceptible.

The **complex domain** involves 'unknown unknowns' (things we don't know that we don't know) where we can use emergent patterns through probing or experimenting (OODA) to ultimately sense (observe) and then respond (act). This domain is commonly characterized by a probe–sense–respond pattern. Consider all the activities you do in your environment that require curiosity and creativity in experimenting; they perhaps require complex choices.

The **chaotic domain** involves the 'unknowable' (things we cannot know) where we can use novel patterns through acting or through exploring or discovering (OODA) to ultimately sense (observe) and respond (act) and to transform the situation from chaos to complexity. This domain is commonly characterized by an act–sense–respond pattern. Consider all the activities you do in your environment that require confidence and courage in exploring or discovering; they perhaps require immediate action.

The complex and chaotic domains presume an unordered reality – a reality that is more volatile, uncertain, complex, and ambiguous and where the relationship between cause and effect is not perceptible.

The Cynefin framework helps us to understand how we orient and decide (as we observe and act) while experiencing reality. More routine activities require more simple choices, expertise requires more complicated choices, curiosity and creativity in experimenting require more complex choices, and confidence and courage in exploring and discovering require more immediate action. Again, consider your life, the opportunities and threats that exist based on your strengths and weaknesses, and how you are orienting and deciding (as you observe and act).

HUMAN MEANINGFULLY PURPOSEFUL ENTERPRISE

Only by integrating the nature of reality with how we interact with reality and how we experience reality can we be successful.

An organization, an enterprise of individuals as a collective, is a social ecosystem. Whether an organization is healthy and thrives is based on people's well-being and performance. Well-being is determined by human functioning – the more functional the people, the more well-being. Performance is determined by efficiency and effectiveness – the more efficient and effective the people, the better the performance.

Human nature (and human beings as social animals) can generally be explored relative to two dimensions: a system dimension and a socio-cultural dimension. Human nature and human endeavours can generally be explored as meaningfully purposeful enterprises. Success emerges from human nature and human dynamics in the context of the human condition.

In a natural state of chaos, the roots of efficiency, effectiveness, and dysfunction are actions and conflict. Intentions orient actions and results are the outcomes of actions. Conflict emerges from natural tensions between intentions, actions, and results. Within a collective, individuals pull from other individuals and create a flow of actions and content. The ultimate results may (or may not) be of value, depending on context. Within a collective, individuals naturally experience conflict as an integral aspect of human nature (and of human beings as social animals). Conflict becomes destructive if and when it escalates into aggression. Conflict ultimately shapes the collective's identity, which is an amalgamation of that which it deems to be its purpose and that which it deems gives it meaning.

Fundamentally, conflict emerges from tensions between collective needs and individual human needs. As conflict escalates into aggression, it fosters dysfunction, which impacts efficiency and effectiveness, which in turn impact identity, value, and so on and depletes people's humanity, natural creativity, and innovation. Fundamentally, the efficiency-and-effectiveness paradigm forms the skeletal backbone that integrates collective needs and individual human needs, and only by reconsidering this paradigm can collectives and individuals amplify people's humanity, natural creativity, and innovation.

Fundamentally, the essential forces influencing collective needs and individual human needs are internal integration and external adaptation.

Thriving requires human organizations or enterprises that work with reality. Many enterprises simply don't work with reality; instead they work with a 'pseudo-reality' conjured up so as to avoid having to work with reality. For organizations to be more human and act as human enterprises, we must reconceive or re-imagine our organizations through a paradigm that appreciates the forces of external adaptation and internal integration as well as our individual and collective humanity.

Well-being involves being human and performance involves thriving. Dysfunction is fundamentally culture; just as individuality is the aggregate of an individual's idiosyncrasies, culture is the aggregate of a collective's idiosyncrasies. Being creatively efficient trumps mere efficiency, and being innovatively effective trumps mere effectiveness, thus integrating individual and collective needs. Intentions, actions, results, flow, and pull blend in co-creation. Aggression is a less artful approach to dealing with conflict. External adaptation blends value (of experiences as an aggregate of products and services), results, and context. Internal adaptation blends identity, purpose, and meaning.

What about strategy? Strategy is embodied throughout – strategy and execution surround thriving. What about leadership? Leadership is embodied throughout – everyone leads from their role and perspective. What about execution? Execution is embodied throughout – everyone engages from their role and perspective.

Individuals and Collectives

As individuals form collectives, which in turn form an enterprise, they sustain their individual identity but engage in a shared identity. Individual and collective identity is expressed through ownership, intentions, and actions.

The enterprise prospers if there is commitment to values and alignment on a cause and, thus, a meaningfully purposeful enterprise within the context of an ecosystem. Meaning motivates, purpose inspires, and meaning and purpose animate, as do motivation and inspiration. This process of animation might be called 'aliveness'.

Identity

Individual identity is defined by our individual values and purpose. Identity encapsulates awareness and ownership, awareness involves being conscious of ourselves and one another, while ownership involves initiative in embracing how we impact and are impacted by one another. Furthermore, identity should not be confused with ego, which is focused only on the self. Awareness has various aspects, including self-awareness, social awareness, and contextual awareness. When we integrate our internal reality and external reality, we commonly experience this as presence. The ability to integrate these aspects and regulate ourselves and our energy is crucial to being more fluid and flow through our circumstances and reality. Again, we have a type of 'heartbeat' that is our rate of individual fluidity and collective flow through our circumstances and reality.

Power can be regarded as one individual's ability to impact another individual by manipulating and influencing the individual, or shaping (manipulating and influencing) the environment around the individual. Shaping is distinct because it does not directly impact the other individual's free will but instead directly impacts the context or environment both individuals share. That is, we all impact each other through our context or environment, but we leave each other's free will or freedom alone. Awareness gives us power, and, for power to be exercised 'well', it requires awareness. One individual's power relates to another individual's freedom. Furthermore, power directs an individual's energy. How little we control our reality.

Collective, or enterprise, identity or culture is defined by our shared values and purpose. In *The Corporate Culture Survival Guide*, Edgar Schein (2009) emphasizes the importance of culture:

> *Culture is a pattern of shared tacit and interconnected assumptions that was learned by a group as it solved its problems of external adaptation and internal integration, that has worked well enough to be considered valid and, therefore, to be taught to new members as the correct way to perceive, think, and feel in relation to those problems.*

Ownership, Intentions, and Impacts

Without impact due to action, there is nothing. Without intention to orient action, there may be nothing. A result is the outcome of intention and orientation, and of action and impact.

What is there without action and impact? Nothing. Actions express 'how'. What is there without intention and orientation? Possibly nothing. Intentions express 'what'. Specifically:

- **Results** express outcomes, bridging intentions, and impacts. A result is a solution, experience, product, or service that the enterprise's clients and customers value.
- **Intentions** include the very requirement for a result and its essential details as well as the goals and objectives needed to realize the result.
- **Actions** include the tasks that will realize the result as well as the tasks that will achieve the goals and objectives.
- **Initiatives** are endeavours with specific actions, intentions, and results.

Consider your life, and how meaningful and purposeful everything is (or is not). What are your (and others') intentions? What are your (and others') impacts? What are your (and others') outcomes? What gives everyone meaning? What gives everyone purpose?

Consider ownership and commitment-based accountability vs. accountability by compulsion:

- an owner or champion of **intentions** expresses 'who' commits and is accountable for intentions (which may be prioritized, sized or estimated, and measured) in relation to results
- an owner or champion of **actions** expresses 'who' commits and is accountable for actions (which may be estimated and measured) in relation to results
- an owner or champion of **dynamics** expresses 'who' commits and is accountable for flow and pull in relation to harmonization.

When an intention owner, action owner, and dynamics owner are flowing and pulling together, they are in partnership (harmoniously); they are casting and continuously re-imagining a vision and are navigating appropriately:

- the **intention owner** champions or engages, and pulls the action owner into the dynamics between them both while discovering what is of value to clients and customers
- the **action owner** champions or engages, and pulls the intention owner into the dynamics between them both while delivering what is of value to clients and customers
- the **dynamics owner** champions or facilitates the flow and pull between the intention owner and action owner, and fosters harmonization by addressing the challenges that may impede the flow and pull between the intention owner and the action owner while discovering and delivering.

In many enterprises, an intention owner is commonly a solutions manager, experience manager, product manager, or service manager. They will own the vision and roadmap for evolving a solution, experience, product, or service relative to the needs of clients and customers. Pulling involves the intention owner seeking content from the action owner and integrating that content in forming intentions. A vision orients and a roadmap integrates time. A vision addresses 'what' and a roadmap addresses 'when'. For example, a vision addresses what the features of a solution are, and a roadmap addresses when a specific feature of a solution will be realized.

In many enterprises, an action owner is commonly a solution team, experience team, product team, or service team that owns the approach to realizing a solution, experience, product, or service. Pulling involves the action owner seeking content from the intention owner and integrating that content in forming actions.

In many enterprises, a dynamics owner is commonly a portfolio, programme, or project manager who owns responsibility for fostering the flow and pull between the intention owner and action owner and for fostering harmonization by addressing the challenges that may impede the flow and pull between the intention owner and action owner while discovering and delivering. Challenges are rooted in our individual, collective, and enterprise identities and the interplay between the individuals and collectives within an enterprise.

Consider your life and ownership. Who are the intention owners? Who are the action owners? Who are the dynamics owners? What is the interplay between the individuals and collectives?

Engagement

In the context of any enterprise, rather than consider 'what is' or 'how to', consider 'why'. Why does it work? Because of the organization? The organization's structure? The organization's processes? The people? The technology? Or something else? Most will answer that it works because of the people. Undoubtedly, people are essential to any human endeavour, but the answer to the question is very rich. Consider why one thing works rather than something else. Mutual, authentic, and appreciative engagement lead to partnership:

- **Engagement** involves meaningful and purposeful participation and creation, rationally, emotionally, and pragmatically. Each individual meaningfully and purposefully participates and contributes from their perspective.
- **Mutuality** involves reciprocity. Everyone co-participates and co-creates. Each individual contributes and confirms other individuals' contributions, and individuals 'dance' and explore together.
- **Authenticity** involves genuineness. Everyone participates genuinely. Each individual's contributions and confirmations genuinely represent them and who they are, their identity. Authenticity is commonly expressed through transparency and trust.
- **Appreciation** involves valuing. Everyone is valued for their participation. Each individual's contributions and confirmations are genuinely valued – that is, their identity is valued. Appreciation is commonly expressed through respect.

If we are truly and sincerely authentic and appreciative, we will be shaped by one another as much as we will shape each other, which fosters a culture of mutual, authentic, and appreciative engagement. Co-participation and co-creation foster affinity among individuals within a collective and among collectives within an enterprise.

Why does one thing work rather than something else? Mutual, authentic, and appreciative engagement is necessary in any meaningful and purposeful human endeavour involving multiple people. That is, co-participation and co-creation must be genuine and valued. This is not easy and requires discipline, endurance, perhaps struggle, and so on.

Consider any successful or less-than successful endeavour. Was there engagement? Was it mutual? Was it authentic? Was it appreciative?

Consider your life in the context of engagement. Are engagements mutual? Are engagements authentic? Are engagements appreciative? Are engagements mutual, authentic, and appreciative within meaningful and purposeful endeavours?

Communication, Cooperation, Coordination, Collaboration, and Co-creation

The various aspects of engagement include communication, cooperation, coordination, collaboration, and co-creation. Navigation focuses on integrating communication, cooperation, coordination, collaboration, and co-creation as a journey of experiences to realize intentions:

- **Communication** focuses on interchanging content to foster collaboration and co-creation.
- **Cooperation** focuses on operating in parallel to foster collaboration and co-creation.
- **Coordination** focuses on regular/rhythmic and ir-regular/intermittent integration points in time for synchronization (operating in parallel and interchanging content), which may be shared transparently as appropriate. Synchronization focuses on irregular/intermittent points in time for coordination. Cadence focuses on regular/rhythmic points in time for coordination.

Collaboration fosters owners working together towards a result, which is a co-creation among owners towards an outcome that integrates intentions and orientation with actions and impacts. Collaboration and

co-creation focus on meaningfully purposeful contribution and confirmation using flow and pull:

- Contribution involves investing content and time (as in a return on investment) based on another collaborator's pull for content at the appropriate time.
- Confirmation involves oversight and attaining a 'return' on content and time (as in a return on investment) based on one's pull for content at the appropriate time.
- Collaborators pull content from one another as needed in time, but they don't push content unnecessarily. Collaborators foster the flow and pull of content as needed, but they don't batch content unnecessarily.

Notice the paradigm shift from batch and push to flow and pull, and how collaborators trigger one another as they integrate through time. Furthermore, collaborators are meaningfully purposeful towards a result.

Consider your life and the various aspects of engagement. Is there more communication, cooperation, coordination, collaboration, or co-creation? And what are the implications towards meaning, purpose, intentions, and impacts?

Teams, Communities, Time, Space, and Harmonization

Teams and communities are the foundation of an enterprise. In many enterprises, an intention owner, an action owner, and a dynamics owner form a team where they focus on results. And, in many enterprises, intention owners, action owners, and dynamics owners form communities where they focus on sharing with one another and learning from one another on how to best advance their craft, integrating what they have learned into their teams.

Time is the universal currency and space is the universal context – time-boxing and cadence are essential. Time cycles in space establish the context for collaboration and co-creation. In many enterprises, an intention owner, an action owner, and a dynamics owner use time-boxing or a window of time to achieve results as well as a cadence for multi-year, yearly, quarterly, monthly, weekly, and perhaps daily events to ensure they are all coordinated. Each time-box may open with a planning event to launch the time-box, have routine events to provide status and synchronization, and close with a review event to demonstrate progress and a retrospective event so as to continuously improve. Otherwise, rhythmic events instead of time-boxing may be used to iteratively and incrementally progress towards achieving results.

Harmonization focuses on adoptable, scalable, and sustainable collaboration and co-creation as everything emerges and reality unfolds. In many enterprises, an intention owner, action owner, and dynamics owner use events to coordinate with each other and other intention owners, action owners, and dynamics owners.

Consider your life, teams, communities, time, space, and harmonization. Are teams and communities internally and externally harmonized (in time and space)? Are owners harmonized (in time and space)?

ANTIFRAGILITY

Reality is perpetually disruptive. Given the nature of reality, how we interact with reality, and how we experience reality, each disruption presents an opportunity or threat based on our strengths and weaknesses. Based on our strengths, if we are more creative and can innovate, we may seize a disruption as an opportunity. Based on our weaknesses, if others are more creative and can innovate, we may address a disruption as a threat. Furthermore, we must consider how we can further develop opportunities and strengths as well as transform weaknesses into strengths and threats into opportunities.

The Triad: Fragile, Robust, and Antifragile

Nassim Nicholas Taleb introduced the concept of antifragility in *Antifragile: Things that Gain from Disorder* (2012), where he distinguished between the fragile, the robust, and the antifragile (the 'Triad'):

> *The fragile wants tranquillity, the antifragile grows from disorder, and the robust doesn't care too much.*

'Antifragility' is a neologism that means 'reverse fragility'. Similarly to how the opposite of negative is positive, the opposite of positive fragility is negative fragility, or 'antifragility'.

FRAGILE, ROBUST, AND ANTIFRAGILE

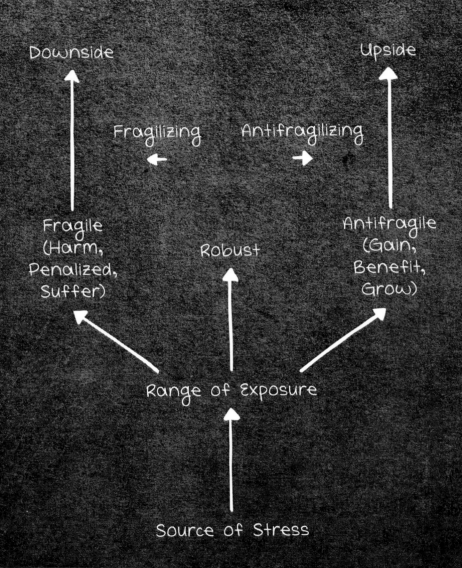

Fragility and antifragility correlate with potential **harm** or **gain** from disorder (or degrees of VUCA). Fragile entities are penalized (or suffer) and antifragile entities benefit (or grow) from exposure to disorder, while robust entities simply remain in their existing state. Disorder (or what Taleb (2012) calls the 'Extended Disorder Family', including chaos, volatility, uncertainty, randomness, variability, chance, the unknown, imperfect and incomplete knowledge, stressors, tensions, errors, entropy, and time) causes stress, which shocks things. Furthermore, we cannot completely track or measure the possibility of these shocks in a VUCA world. Antifragile entities love disorder and a measure of stress. Stress should be considered to be anything that causes energy to be applied or a struggle to unfold in order to advance and achieve an outcome, based on intentions and impact.

Fragility and antifragility are degrees on a spectrum (relative terms, not quite absolute) and are properties of an entity relative to a given situation, limited to a **specific source** (of disorder) and **range of exposure** (or amount of stress). An entity that has more downside in a given situation is more fragile in relation to that specific source and an entity that has more upside in a given situation is more antifragile in relation to that specific source. Fundamentally, a fragile entity wants tranquillity and experiences more downside than upside from disorder; an antifragile entity grows and experiences more upside than downside from disorder (up to a certain level of stress); and a robust entity doesn't care too much. Additionally, the variety and diversity of the sources of stress as well as the amount of stress will determine the fragility and antifragility of an entity. Additionally, the stress must be acute rather than chronic and must be distributed over time so as to only harm the entity to a manageable degree. The degree of stress must be such that the entity can gain from it, and the entity must have sufficient time to recover from the harm and gain from the stress. In addition, by denying or suppressing stress, an entity becomes more fragile, and, with the right amount of stress, an entity becomes more antifragile. Fragilizing, caused by depriving things of disorder and their natural ability to heal, is the process by which things become more fragile. And antifragilizing, which is caused by stressing things (specific source of stress and range of exposure), is the process by which things become more antifragile. Additionally, fragilizing occurs when risk and fragility are transferred between things. It is far more reasonable to figure out whether something is more fragile or more antifragile than it is to calculate the risks and probabilities of rare events that may harm it.

Consider your life and any situations that cause you stress? What is the source of the stress? What level of stress is tolerable and does not impact you? What level of stress, if any, might harm you? What level of stress, if any, might you gain from? Is the stress acute rather than chronic so as to only harm you to a manageable degree? Is the stress distributed over time so as to only harm you to a manageable degree? Do you have sufficient time to recover from the harm and gain from the stress? Is there a variety and diversity of the sources of stress? Is there a variety and diversity of the amount of stress? These are fundamental questions for working with reality.

For example, with physical exercise, if my workout is not strenuous enough, it has no impact; if it is too strenuous, it harms me too much. But, if it is strenuous enough that it has an impact and not so strenuous that it harms me too much, it stresses my muscles with just enough acute harm; with enough recovery time, my muscles recover and become stronger than before. Thus, physical exercise may be antifragilizing. It is fragilizing when it causes too much stress or there is not enough recovery time. It is antifragilizing when it causes a reasonable amount of stress and there is enough recovery time for muscles to develop.

Fundamentally, it is important to determine the specific sources of stress and ranges of exposure that allow us to **leverage stress** to create, discover, and seize opportunities; address threats; develop opportunities and strengths; and transform weaknesses into strengths and threats into opportunities. We must also determine the specific sources of stress and ranges of exposure that allow us to **leverage stress** to not only adjust but also develop our observations, orientation, decisions, and actions. We must always consider the acuteness and distribution over time of the stress and recovery time.

Taleb (2012) explores nature's 'mechanisms of growth and evolution', and in doing so he emphasizes a few key points:

- nature is not 'safe' but rather is 'aggressive in destroying and replacing, in selecting and reshuffling'
- nature is 'opportunistic, ruthless, and selfish'
- nature 'regenerates itself continuously by using, rather than suffering from, random events, unpredictable shocks, stressors, and volatility'.

He them emphasizes that evolution is essential to antifragility – 'evolution, that great expert on antifragility'. Chapter 4 describes the essence of adapting, surviving, evolving, and thriving.

Adapt and Survive or Evolve and Thrive

Today, we experience unprecedented levels of disruption. To survive, we must adapt, but to thrive, we must evolve. Thus, antifragility empowers us to completely embrace reality and emerge stronger, or embrace chaos or embrace disruption, or, as Taleb (2012) expresses it, 'to deal with the unknown, to do things without understanding them – and do them well'.

FRAGILE, ANTI-AGILE, ROBUST, AGILE, AND ANTIFRAGILE

Thrive
(Embrace, Gain,
Evolve (Develop, Build))

Survive
(Confront, Respond,
Adapt (Adjust, Shift))

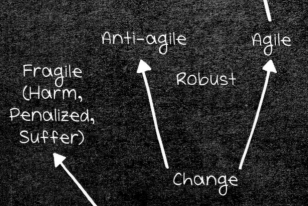

Anti-agile

Agile

Fragile
(Harm,
Penalized,
Suffer)

Robust

Antifragile
(Gain,
Benefit,
Grow)

Change

Disorder

To faithfully interpret antifragility, we must distinguish between the fragile, the anti-agile, the robust, the agile, and the antifragile. The robust doesn't care too much about what it experiences, while the anti-agile and agile focus on change and the fragile and antifragile focus on disorder or disruption. The agile embraces change by adapting to reality while the anti-agile resists change. The antifragile embraces disorder by evolving in the context of reality while the fragile resists disorder and disruption. The difference between agility and antifragility is thus that agility is a change paradigm and antifragility is a chaos paradigm. Embracing change endows us with agility. Embracing chaos endows us with antifragility.

Adaptation is about 'fitness to', which commonly occurs in the moment, while evolution is about 'unfolding from', which commonly occurs over time. Furthermore, evolution generally follows from adaptation, where adaptation is more about confronting and responding to reality while evolution is more about embracing and gaining from reality. Thus, antifragility empowers us to not merely confront reality by adapting and surviving, but also to fully embrace reality by evolving and thriving.

Consider any past situation – with its specific source of stress and range of exposure – and your interaction with it and experience of it. What, how, and why did you gain or lose? Did you merely confront the situation with a response or did you embrace it for gain? Did you merely adjust your interaction with it and experience of it by shifting how you used your existing qualities, or did you develop new ways of interacting and experiencing it by building new qualities? Was the stress acute enough and distributed enough over time? Was there enough time to recover? These are fundamental questions that distinguish between adapting and surviving, and evolving and thriving.

If you are **confronting**, **responding**, or **adjusting** by shifting how you use your qualities, you are adapting and surviving and are thus more agile. If you are **embracing**, **gaining**, or **developing** by building new qualities, you are evolving and thriving and are thus more antifragile. If you fall into neither of these categories, you might be avoiding reality.

Map of the World

Taleb (2012) elaborates his thoughts using the 'Triad' and the 'Map of the World'. The Triad classifies things into the categories of fragile, robust, and antifragile. The Map of the World organizes subjects in relation to the Triad. In a given subject, an item may be categorized using the Triad, and we can consider what we need to do to change its condition so that it gains the characteristics of a different category (that is, becomes more or less fragile or antifragile). The aim is for items to move from fragility towards antifragility, through the reduction of fragility or through the harnessing of antifragility.

For example, in the subject of economic life, Taleb suggests that bureaucrats are fragile and entrepreneurs are antifragile. For a specific individual, we can categorize the individual, and consider what we need to do to help the individual get the characteristics of the latter category and become more antifragile.

In the subject of systems, Taleb suggests that a system confronting concentrated sources of randomness is fragile and a system confronting distributed sources of randomness is antifragile. In the subject of errors, Taleb suggests that the fragile hates mistakes and makes irreversible, large errors while the antifragile loves mistakes and produces reversible, small errors.

Together, Taleb's Triad and Map of the World integrate the various aspects of antifragility around the notion of parts (individuals) progressively (collectives) forming wholes (enterprises), also taking into account their interaction (OODA) with an experience (Cynefin) of reality (VUCA).

After exploring Taleb's Triad and Map of the World, it becomes evident that an antifragile enterprise consists of stakeholders who embrace reality and do not merely confront it, and stakeholders who ensure their aliveness by evolving in engaging with reality and not merely adapting to it. An antifragile enterprise is completely dynamic, at all levels (individual, collective, and enterprise) and in every way. This is the essence of antifragility – a delicate dance between embracing reality and ensuring aliveness.

Individuals, Collectives, and Enterprises

What is the anatomy of an antifragile enterprise?

As stakeholders (individuals and collectives) form an enterprise within an external ecosystem and with an internal ecosystem for the individuals and collectives, the dynamics between the stakeholders (internal dynamics) and the evolution of the enterprise within its ecosystem (external dynamics) determine the antifragility of the enterprise. The dynamics of how **fluid** an individual is, how **flowing** individuals are together as collectives, and how individuals and collectives act together as an enterprise determine the antifragility of the enterprise.

ANTIFRAGILE ENTERPRISE

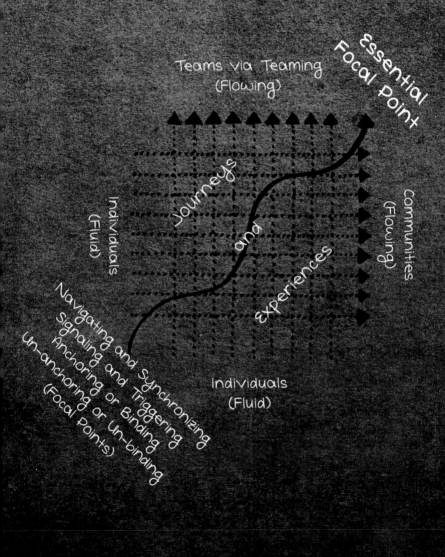

Individuals navigate and synchronize with one another and signal and trigger each other via their dynamics, which include conversations, relationships, and behaviours. An individual's fluidity across collectives and the enterprise determines the individual's antifragility. I'll explore these dynamics in Chapter 2, which covers how individuals embrace reality and ensure their aliveness via their mindsets, questions, leadership, and human dynamics.

> Individual Dynamics =
> Individual Focus
> (Mindsets + Questions + Leadership) +
> Collective Focus
> (Conversations + Relationships + Behaviours)

Collectives navigate and synchronize with one another and signal and trigger each other via 'teaming' and organizing as communities. A collective's flow across an enterprise determines the collective's antifragility. We'll explore teaming and communities in Chapter 3, which covers how collectives embrace reality and ensure their aliveness as groups that work with dysfunction and conflict while teaming and organizing as communities.

> Collective Dynamics =
> Collective Focus
> (Groups + Dysfunctions + Conflict) +
> Enterprise Focus
> (Teaming + Communities)

Thomas Crombie Schelling (2016) developed the idea of focal points (also known as Schelling points) that are solutions, reference points, intersection points, interaction points, connection points, and integration points that people use in their interaction (OODA) with an experience (Cynefin) of reality (VUCA) because they seem natural, special, or relevant to them. Fundamentally, this is why individual identity and cultural identity are important, as they are crucial focal points to determine other focal points. Furthermore, focal points are not static, but are continuously dynamic and change over time.

As individuals and collectives organize around focal points across an enterprise – that is, as they anchor or bind together and as they un-anchor or un-bind from each other – the fluidity of individuals and flow of collectives determine the enterprise's antifragility. Furthermore, in an antifragile enterprise, individuals and collectives don't fixate on anchors but instead leverage them as they navigate.

In Chapter 4, we'll explore how enterprises, composed of individuals and collectives, embrace reality and ensure their aliveness through adaptive cycles and through Crawford Stanley Holling's (2001) concept of 'panarchy' in order to adapt, survive, evolve, and thrive.

Enterprise =
Adaptive Cycles Independently at Every Level +
Panarchy Interdependently across All Levels +
Context or Environment

And, in Chapter 5, we'll explore an actionable road-map for achieving greater antifragility.

The Antifragility Edge =
Embracing Reality + Ensuring Aliveness

Achieving an Antifragility Edge =
Designing and Creating + Evolving and Thriving

Embracing Reality: Seek Opportunities to Thrive

In an antifragile enterprise, what does embracing reality involve?

Embracing reality involves having an empirical world-view and using heuristics regarding external dynamics between stakeholders and reality.

EMBRACING REALITY

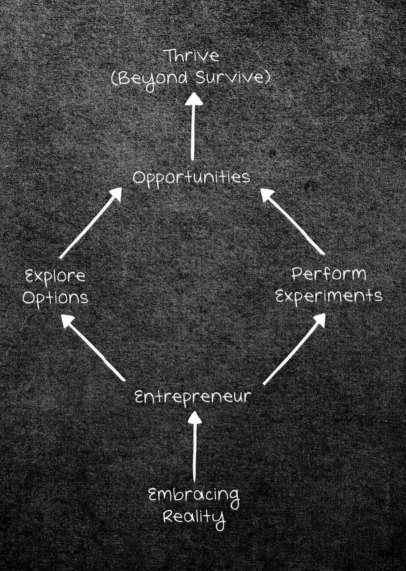

Having an empirical worldview involves understanding the world through our experience of reality rather than understanding the world through a hypothetical understanding of reality. Many individuals, collectives, and enterprises attempt to understand reality through hypothetical models. Rather, we should empirically derive models based on reality and should elaborate them through options and experiments. A theoretical worldview that is not grounded in reality causes fragility.

Heuristics involve simple, practical, expedient, and easy-to-apply rules of thumb for interacting with and understanding reality that are nevertheless accepted to be imperfect. Heuristics can be considered patterns that must be applied in context to be meaningful. Given that we can't understand everything about reality, heuristics allow us to focus on nuances rather than having to keep all details in mind. Details alone don't offer certainty. Precision alone does not offer certainty. Many individuals, collectives, and enterprises attempt to understand reality through idealized rules. Rather, we should derive rules based on our experience of reality and elaborate them through options and experiments. Idealized rules that are not grounded in reality cause fragility.

In considering external dynamics between stakeholders and reality, it is helpful to remember that **entrepreneurs** experiment with options to confront disorder. Entrepreneurs are always exploring and seeking opportunities to enable them to thrive; when they encounter disorder and sufficiently and reasonably struggle, they consider their options and experiment, making small and reversible errors that cause acute stress, distributed over time, with ample recovery time, to enable them to learn and grow.

When stakeholders in enterprises act like entrepreneurs, antifragility is enhanced. As entrepreneurs, we consider our options and experiment to seek opportunities and thrive.

Ensuring Aliveness: Seek Experiences to Evolve

In an antifragile enterprise, what does ensuring aliveness involve?

Ensuring aliveness involves having an essential worldview and using heuristics regarding the internal dynamics between stakeholders.

ENSURING ALIVENESS

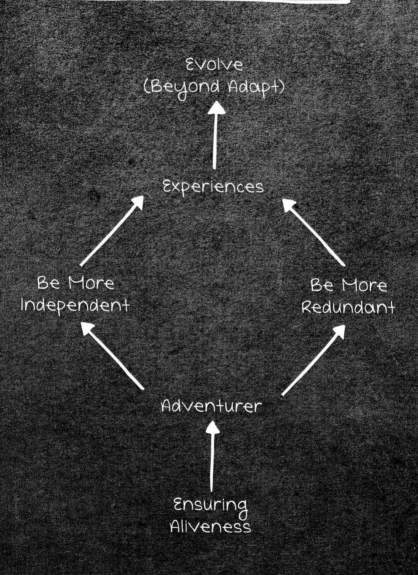

Evolve
(Beyond Adapt)

Experiences

Be More
Independent

Be More
Redundant

Adventurer

Ensuring
Aliveness

Having an essential worldview involves understanding the world through a minimal model of reality rather than understanding the world through an elaborate model of reality. Many individuals, collectives, and enterprises attempt to understand reality through elaborate models. Rather, we should derive minimal models with an essential set of rules and elaborate them through some sense of aliveness. Both under-elaborate and over-elaborate worldviews cause fragility. Similarly, both having too few heuristics and having too many heuristics cause fragility.

In considering internal dynamics between stakeholders, it is helpful to remember that **adventurers** are small, non-specialized, and independent. Adventurers are always exploring and seeking experiences from which to evolve; individually, they don't specialize and are very independent, and, collectively, they don't compromise by specializing or becoming dependent, instead becoming redundant and sharing power.

When we are adventurers, antifragility is enhanced. As adventurers, individually, we don't specialize and are independent in seeking experiences and evolving. As adventurers, we collectively become redundant and share power so as to seek experiences and evolve.

Antifragility: Embracing Reality and Ensuring Aliveness

The essence of antifragility is a delicate dance between embracing reality and ensuring aliveness, where disorder or stress is at the intersection.

Reality influences aliveness and aliveness influences reality. Different understandings of reality, interacting with reality, and experiencing reality emerge from intermingling too little, just enough, or too much reality with too little, just enough, or too much aliveness. The 'wrong' intermingling of reality and aliveness can ultimately lead to death and the 'right' intermingling of reality and aliveness can ultimately lead to growth and being alive – with everything in between, including being numb, under-stimulated, over-stimulated, and so on.

We'll explore this delicate dance between reality and aliveness throughout the book alongside considering how best to foster individual, collective, and enterprise antifragility.

Fundamentally, as a coach, I am a 'micro-stressor' or 'micro-disruptor' who creates micro-degrees of VUCA leveraging reality. Reality is the 'macro-stressor'. I apply my energy to stress individuals, collectives, and enterprises relative to external forces in order for them to survive, thrive, and embrace reality. I apply my energy to stress individuals, collectives, and enterprises relative to internal forces in order for them to adapt, evolve, and ensure their aliveness.

Again, please note that I've removed many specifics and details from the examples so as not to reveal personal or professional information, and have focused instead on essential insights. Additionally, I have intentionally repeated some text in various places so that you can read Chapters 2, 3, 4, and 5 in any order and you can read almost any chapter section in any order after the chapter introduction.

CHAPTER 2

INDIVIDUAL ANTI-FRAGILITY

This chapter explores how individuals operationalize antifragility through their conversations, relationships, and behaviours.

How does an individual **interact with reality** and **experience reality**?

Our interactions with reality and experiences of reality individually are rooted in our conversations, relationships, and behaviours. As individuals, our mindsets, questions, and leadership exemplify our individual identity and our antifragility.

INDIVIDUAL ANTIFRAGILITY

Conversations

Leadership
(Mindsets
and Questions)

Relationships

Behaviours

How does an individual **embrace reality** and thrive as well as **ensure their aliveness** and evolve?

Individuals embrace reality as entrepreneurs who seek opportunities from which to thrive using their conversations, relationships, and behaviours. Individuals ensure their aliveness as adventurers who seek experiences from which to evolve using their conversations, relationships, and behaviours.

How do an **individual's strengths, weaknesses, opportunities, and threats** relate to antifragility?

An individual might evaluate a situation by appraising their strengths and weaknesses from an internal viewpoint and opportunities and threats from an external viewpoint. The individual might explore how to leverage a specific source of stress and range of exposure to:

- create, discover, and seize opportunities
- address threats, maximize strengths, and minimize weaknesses
- develop opportunities and strengths
- transform weaknesses into strengths and threats into opportunities.

How do an **individual's observations, orientation, decisions, and actions** relate to antifragility?

An individual might observe, orient, decide, and act to adapt and survive as well as evolve and thrive. The individual might explore how to leverage a specific source of stress and range of exposure to:

- adjust their observations, orientation, decisions, and actions
- develop their observations, orientation, decisions, and actions.

MINDSETS

In *Mindset: The New Psychology of Success*, Carol Dweck (2007) explores mindsets and distinguishes between the fixed mindset and the growth mindset. I encourage you to explore Dweck's work so as to develop a deeper understanding of mindsets. Here I provide background information regarding mindsets before exploring how they relate to antifragility.

Background

Because antifragility requires us to be entrepreneurs who seek opportunities and thrive as well as adventurers who seek experiences and evolve, our mindset is foundational for our awareness of ourselves and our choices.

Our mindset expresses how we understand our own qualities, as static or dynamic. We naturally experience stress when we understand our own qualities in relation to our circumstances.

An individual with a **fixed mindset** believes that their **qualities are static** and cannot be developed. Such an individual will avoid challenges, give up easily when obstacles are encountered, believe effort is fruitless, ignore negative feedback, be threatened by the success of others, and generally achieve less of their full potential.

An individual with a fixed mindset will not seek experiences or opportunities, and thus is likely to be more fragile.

An individual with a **growth mindset** believes that their **qualities can be developed** and are not static. Such an individual will embrace challenges, persist when obstacles are encountered, believe effort leads to mastery, learn from negative feedback, learn from the success of others, and generally achieve more of their full potential.

An individual with a growth mindset will seek experiences and opportunities, and thus is likely to be more antifragile.

An individual with a fixed mindset can use the following steps to change to a growth mindset: learn to hear their fixed-mindset voice; recognize that they have a **choice**; talk back to that voice with a growth-mindset voice; and take the growth-mindset action.

An individual who recognizes that they have a choice will experience their choices as options, as discussed in Chapter 1. Awareness of oneself and one's choices is a foundation for individual antifragility.

Additionally, the number, variety, diversity, and variation of options must be constrained by the amount of time one has in which to explore those options. Otherwise, one can be fragile in relation to time.

Antifragility

How do mindsets relate to antifragility?

A growth mindset expands an individual's openness to themselves and their options, and antifragility requires entrepreneurs who consider their options and experiment to seek opportunities and thrive as well as adventurers who are independent, redundant, and share power so as to seek experiences and evolve. For these reasons, an individual with a growth mindset is more antifragile than an individual with a fixed mindset.

When coaching individuals on their mindset and choices or options, we focus on challenges and obstacles, specifically those related to conversations, relationships, and behaviours.

Fixed mindset. This individual believed that their qualities were static and could not be developed. I raised awareness of their choices, and suggested that choices are really options that we can exercise within our circumstances. The more options we consider, the more choices we have and the more we can grow.

We identified that they avoided challenges, gave up easily when they encountered obstacles, believed effort was fruitless, ignored negative feedback, was threatened by the success of others, and generally focused on achieving less of their full potential.

I suggested they work with the challenges and obstacles in their conversations, relationships, and behaviours. They began to recognize that their fixed mindset limited their openness to themself and their options.

Growth mindset. This individual believed that their qualities could be developed and were not static. I raised awareness of their choices, and suggested that choices are really options, similarly to the previous example.

We recognized that they embraced challenges, persisted when they encountered obstacles, believed effort leads to mastery, learned from negative feedback, learned from the success of others, and generally focused on achieving more of their full potential.

I encouraged them to use their mindset to expand their options. They began to recognize that their growth mindset expanded their openness to themself and their options.

These examples demonstrate that a fixed mindset limits an individual's openness to themselves and their options and a growth mindset expands an individual's openness to themselves and their options. Therefore, an individual with a growth mindset is more antifragile than an individual with a fixed mindset.

QUESTIONS

In *Change Your Questions, Change Your Life*, Marilee G. Adams (2016) explores mindsets and distinguishes between how the judger mindset uses questions and how the learner mindset uses questions. Here I have provided foundational information on questions and how they relate to antifragility.

Background

Because antifragility requires us to be entrepreneurs who seek opportunities and thrive as well as adventurers who seek experiences and evolve, our mindset is foundational for our awareness of reality and the questions we use.

Our questions express how we understand our circumstances, judging them or learning from them. We naturally experience stress when we understand our circumstances in relation to our qualities.

An individual with a **judger mindset** is more **reactive to circumstances** and uses **judgemental questions** that foster pessimism (reaction), limited possibilities, automatic reactions, and also focus on problems based on negatively judging circumstances. Such questions include: What is wrong? Whose fault is it? Why am I (or are they) such a failure?

An individual with a judger mindset will not seek experiences and will not seek opportunities, and thus is likely to be more fragile.

An individual with a **learner mindset** is more **responsive to circumstances** and considers **unbiased questions** that foster optimism, new possibilities, thoughtful choices, and also focuses on solutions based on unbiased learning about the circumstances. Such questions include: What happed? What can I learn? What is possible? What are my choices?

An individual with a learner mindset will seek experiences and opportunities, and thus is likely to be more antifragile.

An individual with a judger mindset can use switching questions to switch to a learner mindset. Such questions include: Am I judging? How else can I think about this?

An individual who can use questions to be responsive to circumstances rather than reactive to them will experience those questions as experiments, as discussed in Chapter 1. Awareness of reality and of one's questions is a foundation for individual antifragility.

Additionally, the number, variety, diversity, and variation of experiments must be constrained by the amount of time one has in which to perform those experiments. Otherwise, one can be fragile in relation to time.

Antifragility

How do questions relate to antifragility?

A learner mindset expands an individual's openness to reality and experiments, and antifragility involves entrepreneurs who consider their options and experiment to seek opportunities and thrive as well as adventurers who are independent, redundant, and share power to seek experiences and evolve. For these reasons, an individual with a learner mindset is more antifragile than an individual with a judger mindset.

When coaching individuals on their mindset and questions or experiments, we focus on problematic circumstances, specifically those related to conversations, relationships, and behaviours.

Judger mindset. This individual was more reactive to circumstances. I raised awareness of their questions, and suggested that questions are really experiments that we can perform to understand our circumstances. The more experiments we consider, the more questions we can answer and the more we can learn.

We identified that they considered judgemental questions that fostered pessimism and limited possibilities, and they focused on problems based on negatively judging the circumstances.

I suggested they work with their problematic circumstances. They began to recognize that their judger mindset limited their openness to reality and experiments.

Learner mindset. This individual was more responsive to circumstances. I raised awareness of their questions, and suggested that questions are really experiments that we can perform to understand our circumstances, similarly to the previous example.

We recognized that they considered unbiased questions that fostered optimism and new possibilities, and they focused on solutions based on unbiased learning about their circumstances.

I encouraged them to use their mindset to expand their experiments. They began to recognize that their learner mindset expanded their openness to reality and experiments.

These examples demonstrate that a judger mindset limits an individual's openness to reality and experiments and that a learner mindset expands an individual's openness to reality and experiments. Therefore, an individual with a learner mindset is more antifragile than an individual with a judger mindset.

LEADERSHIP

In *Change Intelligence*, Barbara A. Trautlein (2013) explores change leadership styles and distinguishes between coach, visionary, executer, champion, driver, facilitator, and adapter leadership styles. Here I have provided foundational information on change leadership styles and how they relate to antifragility.

Background

Because antifragility requires us to be entrepreneurs who seek opportunities and thrive as well as adventurers who seek experiences and evolve, our leadership style integrates our awareness of ourselves and reality.

Our leadership style expresses our identity and our independence or dependence. It determines how we integrate choices and questions in the form of options and experiments, as discussed earlier in this chapter. We naturally experience stress when we express our identity and our independence or dependence, and integrate choices and questions in the form of options and experiments in relation to our qualities and circumstances.

Every individual has a dominant leadership style that is a mixture of heart (affective/heart-set), head (cognitive/mindset), and hand (behaviours/skill-set) leadership tendencies.

However, individuals do not lead completely from the heart, head, or hands; instead they tend to blend all three.

An individual with a **coach leadership style** has a basic tendency to lead with their heart. They are people-oriented and connect with others emotionally and motivate them.

An individual with a dominant coach leadership style will generally focus their choices and questions on people. This can unintentionally make the individual dependent on people and more fragile in situations that require a focus on purpose or process.

An individual with a **visionary leadership style** has a basic tendency to lead with their head. They are purpose-oriented (why and what) and connect with people cognitively and inspire them.

An individual with a dominant visionary leadership style will generally focus their choices and questions on purpose. This can unintentionally make the individual dependent on purpose and more fragile in situations that require a focus on people or process.

An individual with an **executer leadership style** has a basic tendency to lead with their hands. They are process-oriented (how) and connect with people behaviourally and by being systematic with them.

An individual with a dominant executer leadership style will generally focus their choices and questions on process. This can unintentionally make the individual dependent on process and more fragile in situations that require a focus on people or purpose.

An individual with a **champion leadership style** has a basic tendency to lead with their heart and head.

An individual with a **driver leadership style** has a basic tendency to lead with their head and hands. An individual with a **facilitator leadership style** has a basic tendency to lead with their heart and hands. An individual with an **adapter leadership style** has a basic tendency to lead with their heart, head, and hands.

An individual with a dominant adapter leadership style will generally focus their choices and questions on people, purpose, and process. This can make the individual more independent and thus more antifragile. Furthermore, this also requires that the individual adapt and develop their leadership style.

No one leadership style is inherently better or worse, but each is more or less effective in different situations.

Antifragility

How does leadership relate to antifragility?

An individual's leadership style integrates their awareness of themselves, reality, options, and experiments as well as their independence. Antifragility requires entrepreneurs who consider their options and experiment as well as adventurers who are independent, redundant, and share power. Entrepreneurs seek opportunities and thrive while adventurers seek experiences and evolve. Therefore, an individual's leadership style is crucial in determining their antifragility.

When coaching individuals on their leadership, we explore their leadership styles and blind spots.

Coach leadership style. This individual had a basic tendency to lead with their heart. They were people-oriented and connected with people emotionally and motivated them. We worked together to explore how their focus on people could be problematic and must be balanced with purpose and process.

We identified a few of their subordinates on whom to focus – specifically those who were motivated but not performing. I coached them to work with options and experiments by focusing on the purpose of these people's efforts and the processes they were using.

As a result, they became more aware of their need to focus on purpose and process in addition to people. They began to recognize that their style of leadership determined their awareness of themself and reality, and that their focus on people could make them dependent on people.

Visionary leadership style. This individual had a basic tendency to lead with their head. They were purpose-oriented and connected with people cognitively and inspired them. We explored how their focus on purpose could be problematic and must be balanced with a focus on people and process.

We identified a few goals and objectives on which to focus, specifically related to how they were inspiring others but were not being achieved. I advised them to work with options and experiments by focusing on the people trying to accomplish the goals and objectives and the processes they were using.

As a result, they became more aware of their need to

focus on people and process in addition to purpose. They began to recognize that their style of leadership determined their openness to exploring options and performing experiments, and that their focus on purpose could make them dependent on purpose.

Executer leadership style. This individual had a basic tendency to lead with their hands. They were process-oriented and connected with people behaviourally and by being systematic with them. We explored how their focus on process could be problematic and must be balanced with purpose and people.

We identified a few processes on which to focus, specifically related to how they were systematic but were not being performed. I advised them to work with options and experiments by focusing on the goals and objectives of these processes and the people performing them.

As a result, they became more aware of their need to focus on purpose and people in addition to process. They began to recognize that their focus on process could make them dependent on process.

Adapter leadership style. This individual had a basic tendency to lead with their heart, head, and hands. I coached them to use the appropriate heart, head, and hand tendency based on what needed to be achieved. They began to recognize that their style of leadership determined their awareness of themself and reality and their openness to exploring options and performing experiments. They began to recognize that their tendencies could make them more independent.

These examples demonstrate that using various styles of leadership expands an individual's awareness of themselves and reality as well as their openness to exploring options and performing experiments while becoming more independent. Therefore, such an individual is more antifragile.

CONVERSATIONS

In *Conversational Intelligence*, Judith E. Glaser (2013) explores conversations. Here I provide foundational background information regarding conversations; I encourage you to explore Glaser's work for an even deeper understanding.

Background

Because antifragility requires us to fluidly navigate and synchronize with one another, signal and trigger each other, and anchor or bind together and un-anchor or un-bind from each other, our conversations are foundational to our dynamics, including our interactions with and experiences of reality. And, because antifragility requires us to be entrepreneurs who seek opportunities and thrive, as well as adventurers who seek experiences and evolve, our conversations are foundational for our antifragility.

Options and experiments are the 'currency' through which we seek opportunities as entrepreneurs, and independence and redundancy are the currency through which we seek experiences as adventurers. The more options we have and the more experiments we conduct, the higher our potential for opportunities, which power our ability to thrive. The more independence we have and the more we are redundant and distribute power, the higher our potential for experiences, which power our ability to evolve.

Notice that mindsets, questions, and leadership are foundational to conversations.

Conversations are the foundation for relationships and behaviours. Conversations enable people to connect, navigate through their behaviours, and grow to become more antifragile together. That is, conversations allow:

- co-creating, or being inclusive
- humanizing, or being appreciative and empathetic
- aspiring, or being aspirational and expanding
- navigating, or fostering collaboration and sharing
- generating next-generation thinking and wonder
- expressing, or developing and encouraging
- synchronizing, or fostering commitment.

In **transactional conversations** we focus on **giving and receiving information** to confirm what we know. Individuals in such a conversation will exchange information by telling and asking one another. An individual in a transactional conversation is not open to influence and is oriented towards informing by interacting with other individuals.

Transactional conversations are generally valuable for performing experiments as individuals exchange information by telling and asking one another. Furthermore, these conversations create a dependency between individuals where one individual depends on another individual for information.

In **positional conversations** we focus on **persuading and influencing** to defend what we know.

Individuals in such a conversation will exchange power by advocating and inquiring of one another. An individual in a positional conversion has a desire to influence and is oriented towards persuading by interacting with other individuals.

Positional conversations are generally valuable for performing experiments as individuals exchange power by advocating and inquiring of one another. Furthermore, these conversations create a dependency between individuals where one individual depends on another individual and must influence the other individual.

In **transformational conversations** we focus on **exploring** to discover what we don't know. Individuals in such a conversation will exchange energy by sharing and discovering with one another. An individual in a transformational conversation is open to influence and is oriented towards co-creating by interacting with other individuals.

Transformational conversations are generally valuable for exploring options as individuals exchange energy by sharing and discovering with one another. Furthermore, these conversations create a dependency between individuals where the individuals depend on one another to co-create together; they also create redundancy and distribute power.

No one type of conversation is inherently better or worse, but each is more or less effective in different situations.

An individual who uses transactional, positional, and transformational conversations will generally balance – and naturally experience stress when balancing the various types of conversations – their ability to explore options, perform experiments, be redundant, distribute their power, and be independent. This can make the individual more antifragile.

Antifragility

How do conversations foster antifragility?

An individual's conversations play a crucial role in their ability to explore options, perform experiments, be redundant, distribute their power, and be independent. Antifragility requires entrepreneurs who consider their options and experiment as well as adventurers who are independent, redundant, and share power. Entrepreneurs seek opportunities and thrive while adventurers seek experiences and evolve. Therefore, an individual's conversations are crucial in determining their antifragility.

When coaching individuals on their conversations, we focus on opportunities to seize or develop, strengths to maximize or develop, weaknesses to minimize or transform into strengths, and threats to transform into opportunities.

Transactional conversations. This individual focused on giving and receiving information to confirm what they knew. They were not open to influence and were oriented towards informing other individuals. We worked together to explore how their focus on transactional conversations could be problematic and must be balanced with positional and transformational conversations.

First, we focused on informing people to address opportunities, strengths, weaknesses, and threats. Then, I stressed them so as to encourage them to focus on those opportunities, strengths, weaknesses, and threats that could be addressed through persuading people or co-creating with people.

As a result, they began to recognize that their conversations determined their ability to explore options and perform experiments.

Positional conversations. This individual focused on persuading and influencing to defend what they knew. They had a desire to influence and were oriented towards persuading other individuals. We worked together to explore how their focus on positional conversations could be problematic and must be balanced with transactional and transformational conversations.

First, we focused on persuading people to address opportunities, strengths, weaknesses, and threats. Then, I stressed them so as to encourage them to focus on those opportunities, strengths, weaknesses, and threats that could be addressed through informing people or co-creating with people.

As a result, they began to recognize that their conversations determined their ability to explore options and perform experiments, and that their focus on persuading and influencing to defend what they knew could make them more dependent.

Transformational conversations. This individual focused on exploring to discover what they didn't know. They were open to influence and were oriented towards co-creating with other individuals. We explored how their focus on transformational conversations could be problematic and must be balanced with transactional and positional conversations.

First, we focused on those opportunities, strengths, weaknesses, and threats that could be addressed through co-creating with people or through exploring. Then, I coached them to focus on those opportunities, strengths, weaknesses, and threats that could be addressed through informing people or persuading people.

As a result, they began to recognize that their conversations determined their ability to explore options and perform experiments, and that their focus on exploring to discover what they didn't know could make them more dependent. They also began to recognize that they could foster redundancy and distribute their power using various conversations.

Transactional, positional, and transformational conversations. This individual used all types of conversations. I coached them to use the appropriate conversation based on what needed to be achieved. They began to recognize that using various conversations determined their ability to explore options and perform experiments as well as foster redundancy and distribute their power while being more independent.

These examples demonstrate that an individual who can use various types of conversations can explore options, perform experiments, foster redundancy, and distribute their power while being more independent. Therefore, such an individual is more antifragile.

RELATIONSHIPS

In *Tribal Leadership*, Dave Logan, John King, and Halee Fischer-Wright (2011) explore tribes, culture, and relationships. Here I provide background information regarding relationships and how they relate to antifragility, but I encourage you to explore Logan, King, and Fischer-Wright's work for an even deeper understanding.

Background

Because antifragility requires us to fluidly navigate and synchronize with one another, signal and trigger each other, and anchor or bind together and un-anchor or un-bind from each other, our relationships are foundational to our dynamics, including our interactions with and experiences of reality. And, because antifragility requires us to be entrepreneurs who seek opportunities and thrive as well as adventurers who seek experiences and evolve, our relationships are foundational for our antifragility.

Again, options and experiments are the 'currency' through which we seek opportunities as entrepreneurs and opportunities to thrive, and independence and redundancy are the currency through which we seek experiences as adventurers and opportunities to evolve.

Notice that mindsets, questions, and leadership are foundational to relationships.

A tribe is a naturally formed group, a basic sociological unit. Every tribe has a dominant culture. A tribe's culture emerges from language, behaviour, and relationship structures. A tribe's culture can be identified as a stage on a scale of one to five. A leader builds a tribe by upgrading its culture. A leader nudges using language; by changing the language in a tribe, the leader changes the tribe itself.

At **stage one**, people are alienated from each other. They use their relationships to undermine one another; their behaviour expresses despairing hostility and their language expresses the idea that 'life sucks'. To upgrade a tribe at stage one, a leader intervenes by helping people to recognize and appreciate any positive aspects of life.

At **stage two**, people are separate from each other. Their relationships are ineffective; their behaviour is that of apathetic victims and their language expresses the idea 'my life sucks'. To upgrade a tribe at stage two, a leader intervenes by helping individuals to actualize themselves through efforts and results that can be accomplished individually, fostering confidence and **independence**, and by helping individuals to form dyadic (two-individual) relationships. Sometimes this confidence is experienced by others as arrogance (vs. humbleness).

At **stage three**, people experience personal domination of one member over others. Relationships are established for their usefulness; people's behaviour is that of lone warriors and their language expresses 'I'm great (and you're not)'. They form **dyadic relationships**. To upgrade a tribe at stage three, a leader intervenes by helping individuals to actualize themselves through efforts and results that require a team, fostering confidence and

interdependence, and by helping individuals to form triads. Sometimes this confidence is experienced by others as arrogance.

Dyadic relationships are the basis of stage three. At this stage, people form dyadic relationships. Dyadic relationships involve one-on-one conversations where the other person feels commoditized and valued only for their service or information. At this stage, people (hubs) foster relationships where others (spokes) are **dependent** on them.

An individual who is at stage three and who forms dyadic relationships can use their relationships to explore options and perform experiments. While these relationships create dependencies between individuals, the individual's stage-three independence counters the dependence caused by the relationships.

The **epiphany** is the journey from stage three to stage four, where a person is awakened to an ability to reflect on their core assumptions and becomes aware of deeper insights. The person realizes 'I am because we are' and shifts from 'I' and dyadic relationships to 'we' and triadic (three-legged) relationships of people where there is a pure focus on the tribe.

At **stage four**, people experience stable partnerships where their relationships are important, their behaviour expresses tribal pride, and their language expresses 'we're great (and they're not)'. They form **triadic relationships** around core values (or meaning, as discussed in Chapter 1) and a noble cause (or purpose, as discussed in Chapter 1). Core values fuel a tribe; they are what the tribe 'stands for'. A tribe identifies and leverages its core values.

A noble cause is the direction the tribe is heading towards; it is what the tribe 'lives for'. A tribe aligns on a noble cause. To stabilize a tribe at stage four, a leader fosters finding and leveraging commitment to core values, aligning on a noble cause, establishing triadic relationships, and building a strategy.

Triadic relationships are the basis of stage four. At this stage, people form triadic relationships. Triads foster relationships between two other people based on core values and mutual self-interest. This results in loyalty and followership towards the individual fostering the relationship.

Triadic relationships involve three parts, where each part is responsible for the quality of the relationship between the other two parts. That's not to say that one part is responsible for the other two parts, but rather that it is responsible for the quality of the relationship in between the other two parts. At this stage, people foster relationships where others are **interdependent** on each other and unified by their core values and noble cause.

At stage four, a tribe uses a **strategy** with outcomes, assets, and behaviours to advance its cause.

An individual who is at stage four and who forms triadic relationships can use their relationships to explore options and perform experiments. While these relationships create dependencies in the form of interdependencies between individuals, the individual's stage-four triadic relationships counter the dependence and they also create redundancy and distribute power.

At **stage five**, people experience a team of stable partnerships where their relationships are vital; their behaviour expresses innocent wonderment and their language expresses the idea that 'life is great'; and they form networked, triadic relationships.

An individual who uses their dyadic and triadic relationships will generally balance – and naturally experience stress when balancing the various types of relationships – their ability to explore options, perform experiments, be redundant, distribute their power, and be independent. This can make the individual more antifragile.

Antifragility

How do relationships foster antifragility?

An individual's relationships play a crucial role in their ability to explore options, perform experiments, be redundant, distribute their power, and be independent. Antifragility requires entrepreneurs who consider their options and experiment as well as adventurers who are independent, redundant, and share power. Entrepreneurs seek opportunities and thrive while adventurers seek experiences and evolve. Therefore, an individual's relationships are crucial in determining their antifragility.

When coaching individuals on their relationships, we focus on opportunities to seize or develop, strengths to maximize or develop, weaknesses to minimize or transform into strengths, and threats to transform into opportunities.

Stage two. This individual experienced being separate from others. They had ineffective relationships and they behaved like a victim. We worked together to explore their disconnectedness from others and how they could actualize themself through efforts and results that could be accomplished individually, thus fostering their confidence and independence. We also explored how they could form dyadic relationships. Notice that, in many ways, I was acting as a tribal leader.

Then, I suggested they focus on those opportunities, strengths, weaknesses, and threats that could be addressed through dyadic relationships.

As a result, they became more aware of being disconnected from others.

Stage three. This individual experienced being dominated by others or dominating others. They had established relationships for their usefulness, behaved as a lone warrior or with independence, and formed dyadic relationships. We worked together to explore their being dominated by others or dominating others, and how they could actualize themself through efforts and results that require a team; this fostered their confidence and interdependence. We also explored how they could form triadic relationships. Notice that, in many ways, I was acting as a tribal leader.

We first considered their dyadic relationships to address opportunities, strengths, weaknesses, and threats. Then, I stressed them so as to encourage them to focus on those opportunities, strengths, weaknesses, and threats that could be addressed through triadic relationships.

As a result, they became more aware of being dominating.

They began to recognize that their dyadic relationships could make them more dependent but that their stage-three independence offered balance.

Stage four. This individual experienced being in partnership with others. They had established relationships for their importance, behaved with group pride or with interdependence, and formed triadic relationships. We worked together to explore their partnerships and how they could foster commitment to values and alignment on a cause, establish triadic relationships, and build a strategy. Notice that, in many ways, I was acting as a tribal leader.

We first considered their triadic relationships to address opportunities, strengths, weaknesses, and threats. Then, I coached them to focus on those opportunities, strengths, weaknesses, and threats that could be addressed through dyadic relationships.

As a result, they became more aware of the need to balance all types of relationships. They began to recognize that their interdependence could make them more dependent but that their stage-four triadic relationships offered balance. They also began to recognize that they could foster redundancy and distribute their power using various relationships.

Dyadic and triadic relationships. This individual used all types of relationships. I coached them to use the appropriate relationship based on what needed to be achieved. They began to recognize that using various relationships determined their ability to explore options and perform experiments as well as foster redundancy and distribute their power while being more independent.

These examples demonstrate that an individual who can use various types of relationships can explore options, perform experiments, foster redundancy, and distribute their power while being more independent. Therefore, such an individual is more antifragile.

BEHAVIOURS

In *Viral Change*, Leandro Herrero (2008) explores change and behaviours. I encourage you to explore Herrero's work for a deeper understanding of behaviours; here I provide foundational background information regarding behaviours before exploring how they relate to antifragility.

Background

Because antifragility requires us to fluidly navigate and synchronize with one another, signal and trigger each other, and anchor or bind together and un-anchor or un-bind from each other, our behaviours are foundational to our dynamics, including our interactions with and experiences of reality. And, because antifragility requires us to be entrepreneurs who seek opportunities and thrive as well as adventurers who seek experiences and evolve, our behaviours are foundational for our antifragility.

Again, options and experiments are the 'currency' through which we seek opportunities as entrepreneurs and opportunities to thrive; independence and redundancy are the currency through which we seek experiences as adventurers and opportunities to evolve.

Notice that mindsets, questions, and leadership are foundational to behaviours.

Viral change involves the orchestration of change

using five disciplines – that is, a social infection of behavioural change.

The **behaviours** discipline involves a **small and non-negotiable set of visible behaviours**. Fundamentally, this discipline determines what the desired behaviours should be. The **stories** discipline involves **socially reinforcing stories** that accelerate change rather than traditional presentations. The **leadership** discipline involves **distributed leadership** that fosters change rather than traditional organizational-chart leadership.

An individual who uses the behaviours discipline will actualize the other disciplines. Conversations and relationships need to translate into decisions and actions that have an impact towards intentions.

The **influence** discipline involves **scalable peer-to-peer influence** (vs. hierarchical influence) that mobilizes change. Fundamentally, this discipline leverages the power of peer-to-peer relationships as well as socially reinforcing stories and distributed leadership, similarly to how Logan, King and, Fischer-Wright (2011) describe relationships in *Tribal Leadership*.

The influence discipline integrates tribal leadership, individual antifragility gained through relationships, and behaviours.

The **social network** discipline involves **informal social networks** that nurture change. Fundamentally, this discipline leverages the power of informal conversations as well as socially reinforcing stories and distributed leadership, similarly to how Glaser (2013) describes conversations in *Conversational Intelligence*.

The social network discipline integrates conversational intelligence, individual antifragility gained through conversations, and behaviours.

An individual who uses behaviour integrated with stories, leadership, relationships, and conversations will generally balance – and naturally experience stress when balancing a variety of behaviours – their ability to explore options, perform experiments, be redundant, distribute their power, and be independent. This can make the individual more antifragile.

Antifragility

How do behaviours foster antifragility?

An individual's behaviours play a crucial role in their ability to explore options, perform experiments, be redundant, distribute their power, and be independent. Antifragility requires entrepreneurs (who consider their options and experiment) as well as adventurers (who are independent, redundant, and share power). Entrepreneurs seek opportunities and thrive while adventurers seek experiences and evolve. Therefore, an individual's behaviours are crucial in determining their antifragility.

When coaching individuals on their behaviours, we focus on opportunities to seize or develop, strengths to maximize or develop, weaknesses to minimize or transform into strengths, and threats to transform into opportunities.

Behaviour. This individual focused on behaviour. I raised awareness of their (sometimes extreme) focus on behaviour and the blind spots it might create. They focused on a small and non-negotiable set of visible behaviours.

We first considered their specific behaviours so as to address opportunities, strengths, weaknesses, and threats. Then, I coached them to focus on those opportunities, strengths, weaknesses, and threats that could be addressed through specific social stories or distributed leadership and through specific peer-to-peer relationships and informal conversations. I coached them to foster social stories, distributed leadership, peer-to-peer relationships, and informal conversations.

As a result, they became more aware of their focus on specific behaviours and the need to balance all disciplines. They began to recognize that their behaviours determined their ability to explore options and perform experiments, and that their focus on specific behaviours could make them more dependent. Additionally, they began to recognize that, by using a variety of behaviours, they could foster redundancy and distribute their power.

Social stories and distributed leadership to accelerate and foster behaviour. This individual focused on stories and leadership. I raised awareness of their (sometimes extreme) focus on stories and leadership and the blind spots it might create. They focused on socially reinforcing stories and distributed leadership.

We first considered their specific social stories and distributed leadership so as to address opportunities, strengths, weaknesses, and threats. Then, I coached them to focus on those opportunities, strengths, weaknesses, and threats that could be addressed through specific behaviours and through specific peer-to-peer relationships and informal conversations. I emphasized behaviours, peer-to-peer relationships, and informal conversations.

As a result, they became more aware of their focus on specific social stories and distributed leadership and the need to balance all disciplines. They began to recognize that their social stories and distributed leadership determined their ability to explore options and perform experiments, and that their focus on specific social stories and distributed leadership could make them more dependent.

Peer-to-peer relationships and informal conversations to mobilize and nurture behaviour. This individual focused on relationships and conversations. I raised awareness of their (sometimes extreme) focus on relationships and conversations and the blind spots it might create. They focused on peer-to-peer influence and informal social networks.

We first considered their specific peer-to-peer relationships and informal conversations so as to address opportunities, strengths, weaknesses, and threats. Then, I coached them to focus on those opportunities, strengths, weaknesses, and threats that could be addressed through specific behaviours and through specific social stories or distributed leadership. I emphasized behaviours, social stories, and distributed leadership.

As a result, they became more aware of their focus on specific peer-to-peer relationships and informal conversations and the need to balance all disciplines. They began to recognize that their peer-to-peer relationships and informal conversations determined their ability to explore options and perform experiments, and that their focus on specific peer-to-peer relationships and informal conversations could make them more dependent.

Behaviour, social stories, distributed leadership, peer-to-peer relationships, and informal conversations. This individual used all disciplines. I coached them to use the appropriate disciplines based on what needed to be achieved. They began to recognize that using a variety of behaviours, social stories, distributed leadership, peer-to-peer relationships, and informal conversations determined their ability to explore options and perform experiments as well as foster redundancy and distribute their power while being more independent.

These examples demonstrate that an individual who can use a variety of behaviours, social stories, distributed leadership, peer-to-peer relationships, and informal conversations can explore options, perform experiments, foster redundancy, and distribute their power while being more independent. Therefore, such an individual is more antifragile.

ACHIEVING INDIVIDUAL ANTIFRAGILITY

To achieve greater antifragility, an individual must interact with reality and experience reality through their conversations, relationships, and behaviours. They must embrace reality and thrive in it. They must ensure they are evolving based on their strengths, weaknesses, opportunities, and threats as well as observations, orientation, decisions, and actions. As individuals, our mindsets, questions, and leadership exemplify our individual identity and our antifragility.

To achieve greater antifragility, individuals navigate and synchronize with one another and signal and trigger each other via their dynamics. These include conversations, relationships, and behaviours. An individual's fluidity across collectives and the enterprise determines the individual's antifragility.

Antifragility requires us to be entrepreneurs and adventurers. As entrepreneurs, we consider our options and experiment to seek opportunities and thrive. As adventurers, we individually don't specialize and are very independent in seeking experiences and evolving. As adventurers, we collectively become redundant and share power to seek experiences and evolve.

Herein is a summary of the sections in this chapter:

- **Mindsets**: A fixed mindset limits an individual's openness to themselves and their options. A growth mindset expands an individual's openness to themselves and their options.

- **Questions**: A judger mindset limits an individual's openness to reality and experiments. A learner mindset expands an individual's openness to reality and experiments.

- **Leadership**: Using various styles of leadership expands an individual's awareness of themself and reality as well as their openness to explore options and perform experiments while being more independent.

- **Conversations, relationships, and behaviours**: An individual who can use various types of conversations, various types of relationships, and a variety of behaviours, social stories, distributed leadership, peer-to-peer relationships, and informal conversations can explore options, perform experiments, foster redundancy, and distribute their power while being more independent.

An individual's mindset, questions, and leadership while conversing, relating, and behaving over time empowers the individual to achieve greater antifragility.

Consider an individual with a tendency to use various types of conversations, various types of relationships, and a variety of behaviours. Coaching this individual, I recognized and appreciated the 'mystery' of their individuality and individual identity. I raised awareness of their conversations, relationships, behaviours, mindset, questions, and leadership. When some of their initiatives were challenged, I observed and became increasingly aware of their strengths, weaknesses, opportunities, and threats. We worked together to explore the initiatives, challenges, and situations as well as their strengths, weaknesses, opportunities, and threats. Working with our awareness, first, we focused on those strengths, weaknesses, opportunities, and threats that could be addressed with minimal stress while accomplishing what needed to be achieved. Second, working with our awareness, we then focused on creating and discovering opportunities. Finally, working with our awareness, I coached them to focus on those strengths, weaknesses, opportunities, and threats that involved progressively more stress while accomplishing what needed to be achieved. As I stressed them, they became more aware of themself and everything around them. They began to become more antifragile.

In all of the cases throughout this chapter, stress is related to the individual's mindset, questions, leadership, conversations, relationships, and behaviours; ultimately it helps the individual to:

- create, discover, develop, and seize opportunities
- address threats and transform them into opportunities
- maximize and develop strengths
- minimize weaknesses and transform them into strengths
- adjust and develop observations, orientation, decisions, and actions.

While Dweck (2007), Adams (2016), Trautlein (2013), Glaser (2013), Logan, King and, Fischer-Wright (2011), and Herrero (2008) respectively focus on individuals' mindsets, questions, leadership, conversations, relationships, and behaviours, there are other works that may be of value. However, I have found these to be demonstrably beneficial in fostering antifragility in practice.

CHAPTER 3

COLLECTIVE ANTI-FRAGILITY

Thishis chapter explores how collectives operationalize antifragility through teaming and communities.

How does a collective **interact with reality** and **experience reality**?

Our interactions with reality and experiences of reality are rooted in our teaming and communities. As collectives, how we work as groups, work with dysfunction, and work with conflict exemplify our collective identity and our antifragility.

COLLECTIVE ANTIFRAGILITY

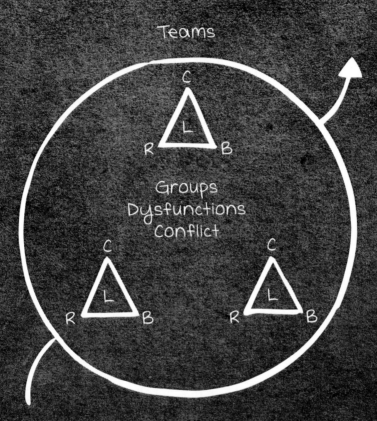

L = Leadership (Mindsets and Questions)
C = Conversations
R = Relationships
B = Behaviours

How does a collective **embrace reality** and thrive as well as **ensure its aliveness** and evolve?

Collectives embrace reality as entrepreneurs (who seek opportunities from which to thrive) by teaming. Collectives ensure their aliveness as adventurers (who seek experiences from which to evolve) by organizing as communities.

How do a **collective's strengths, weaknesses, opportunities, and threats** relate to **antifragility**?

A collective might approach a situation by assessing its strengths and weaknesses from an internal viewpoint and assessing its opportunities and threats from an external viewpoint. The collective might explore how to leverage a specific source of stress and range of exposure to create, discover, develop, and seize opportunities; address threats and transform them into opportunities; maximize and develop strengths; and minimize weaknesses and transform them into strengths.

How do a **collective's observations, orientation, decisions, and actions** relate to **antifragility**?

A collective might observe, orient, decide, and act to adapt and survive as well as evolve and thrive. The collective might explore how to leverage a specific source of stress and range of exposure to adjust and develop its observations, orientation, decisions, and actions to adapt and survive as well as evolve and thrive.

GROUPS

Here I have provided foundational information regarding groups and explored how they relate to antifragility. However, I encourage you to explore *Developmental Sequence in Small Groups* by Bruce Wayne Tuckman (1965). Tuckman explores group development by distinguishing between the five stages of group development — forming, storming, norming, performing, and adjourning — and across two realms: interpersonal or group structure and task activity.

Background

Because antifragility requires us to be entrepreneurs who seek opportunities and thrive as well as adventurers who seek experiences and evolve, a collective's ability to work as a group or unit is foundational for its dynamics, including its interaction with reality and experience of reality.

Groups have five stages of development across two realms. Groups naturally experience stress when working with the five stages and two realms.

The **interpersonal or group structure realm** focuses on relationships between group members. Fundamentally, this realm focuses on relationships, similarly to how Logan, King and, Fischer-Wright (2011) describe relationships in *Tribal Leadership*. The **task activity realm** focuses on the interactions or behaviours between group members. Fundamentally, this realm focuses on behaviours, similarly to how Herrero (2008) describes behaviours in *Viral Change*. The interpersonal or group structure realm and the task activity realm are integrated as group members engage in conversations. Fundamentally, the two realms are integrated through conversations, similarly to how Glaser (2013) describes conversations in *Conversational Intelligence*.

A collective or group integrates individuals, including their conversations, relationships, and behaviours. A group's collective antifragility emerges from integrating each individual's antifragility.

The **forming stage** focuses on **when individuals engage together to form a group**. During this stage, individuals explore and discover their dependence on one another and their orientation towards the group's goals and objectives. A collective in the forming stage has not yet integrated all of the individuals.

The **storming stage** focuses on **conflict**. During this stage, individuals divergently explore and discover how best to relate to one another and how best to behave with one another towards accomplishing the group's goals and objectives. Conflict emerges, given that each individual has their own identity.

The **norming stage** focuses on **cohesion**. During this stage, individuals converge towards how best to relate to one another and how best to behave with one another towards accomplishing the group's goals and objectives. Conflict is addressed as the group gains cohesion and forms its own identity.

A collective in the storming stage or norming stage has integrated all of its individuals. That is, the individuals in the collective use conflict and cohesion to explore options and perform experiments together and to be redundant and disturb power among themselves. Conflict and cohesion are what fuel a collective. Conflict alone or cohesion alone does not fuel a collective. Conflict and cohesion are the foundation for collective antifragility.

The **performing stage** focuses on **performance**. During this stage, the group performs towards accomplishing its goals and objectives. Conflict is addressed and cohesion is maintained as the group performs.

A collective in the performing stage has integrated all of its individuals. That is, the individuals in the collective use conflict and cohesion to explore options and perform experiments together and to be redundant and disturb power among themselves as individuals apply their energy towards the collective's intentions, expressed as goals and objectives. While conflict and cohesion are necessary, they are not sufficient; intentionality is also necessary for collective antifragility. Furthermore, a focus on performance creates a dependency between individuals where the individuals depend on one another.

The **adjourning stage** is when individuals disengage and disband the group. During this stage, individuals explore and discover what is next for them individually.

Antifragility

How do groups relate to antifragility?

A collective where individuals can work as a group plays a crucial role in the individuals' ability to explore options, perform experiments, be redundant, and distribute power. Antifragility requires entrepreneurs who consider their options and experiment as well as adventurers who are independent, redundant, and share power. Entrepreneurs seek opportunities and thrive while adventurers seek experiences and evolve. Therefore, the ability of a collective's individuals to work as a group is crucial in determining the collective's antifragility.

When coaching collectives, we focus on opportunities, strengths, weaknesses, and threats as they work in groups.

Forming stage. This collective was focused on dependence and orientation, and involved individuals who were exploring their dependence on one another and their orientation towards the group's goals and objectives.

I suggested the collective employ more dependence and orientation, and as a result its members became more aware of their need for conflict. The collective began to recognize that getting past the forming stage was crucial.

Storming stage. This collective was focused on conflict and individual identity, and involved individuals who were divergently exploring how to relate to one another and how to behave with one another while accomplishing the collective's goals and objectives. We worked together to explore the use of conflict.

Then, I coached the collective to focus on those opportunities, strengths, weaknesses, and threats that involved progressively more conflict.

As I stressed the collective so as to encourage it to use more conflict, its members became more aware of their need for cohesion.

Norming stage. This collective was focused on cohesion and collective identity, and involved individuals who were converging towards how to relate to one another and how to behave with one another while accomplishing the collective's goals and objectives. We explored cohesion.

Then, I coached the collective to focus on those opportunities, strengths, weaknesses, and threats that involved progressively more cohesion.

As I stressed the collective so as to encourage it to use more cohesion, its members became more aware of their need for conflict.

Performing stage. This collective was focused on conflict, cohesion, and shared identity, and involved individuals who were maintaining how to relate to one another and how to behave with one another while accomplishing the collective's goals and objectives. We worked together to explore performing.

We first considered integrating conflict and cohesion to address opportunities, strengths, weaknesses, and threats. Then, I coached the collective to focus on those opportunities, strengths, weaknesses, and threats that involved progressively more conflict and cohesion.

As I coached the collective to confront more conflict and cohesion, its members became more aware of their performance. The collective began to recognize that getting to the performing stage was crucial in order to explore options and perform experiments together as well as to foster redundancy and distribute power. The collective's members began to realize that a focus on performance could make them more dependent on one another.

These examples demonstrate that a collective where individuals work as a group can focus on options, experiments, redundancy, and power. Therefore, such a collective is more antifragile.

DYSFUNCTIONS

In *The Five Dysfunctions of a Team*, Patrick Lencioni (2002) explores five distinct issues that form an interrelated model for cohesive groups or teams. Here, I explore these issues briefly in relation to antifragility.

Background

Because antifragility requires us to be entrepreneurs who seek opportunities and thrive as well as adventurers who seek experiences and evolve, a collective's ability to work with dysfunction is foundational for its dynamics, including its interaction with reality and experience of reality.

Groups coalesce when they have addressed five distinct issues. Groups naturally experience stress when working with the five distinct issues.

The first issue involves an **absence of trust** among group members. This issue is rooted in individuals being unwilling to be vulnerable within the group. Instead, individuals must be genuinely open with one another about their strengths and weaknesses.

The second issue involves a **fear of conflict** due to an absence of trust. This issue stifles constructive conflict and preserves artificial harmony. Instead, individuals must engage in working with conflict.

A collective confronting trust and conflict issues is really exploring how best to integrate its individuals together to form a collective. This is similar to the forming stage discussed in the Groups section of this chapter. The collective must integrate conflict and cohesion so that the individuals in the collective explore options and perform experiments together and become redundant and disturb power among themselves.

The third issue involves a **lack of commitment** due to a fear of conflict. This issue fosters a lack of clarity and buy-in among individuals. Instead, individuals must commit to decisions and actions.

The fourth issue involves **avoidance of accountability** due to a lack of commitment. This issue fosters hesitance of individuals to hold one another accountable. Instead, individuals must hold each other accountable for delivering against decisions and actions.

The fifth issue involves **inattention to results** due to an avoidance of accountability. This issue fosters individuals putting their needs above the group's needs. Instead, individuals must focus on achieving collective results.

A collective confronting commitment, accountability, and results issues is really exploring how individuals can best apply their energy towards the collective's intentions as individuals explore options and perform experiments together and become redundant and disturb power among themselves. This is similar to the performing stage (integrating the storming and norming stages), discussed in the Groups section of this chapter. Furthermore, a focus on commitment, accountability, and results creates a dependency between individuals where the individuals depend on one another.

Antifragility

How does dysfunction relate to antifragility?

A collective where individuals can work with dysfunction plays a crucial role in the individuals' ability to explore options, perform experiments, be redundant, and distribute power. Antifragility requires entrepreneurs who consider their options and experiment as well as adventurers who are independent, redundant, and share power. Entrepreneurs seek opportunities and thrive while adventurers seek experiences and evolve. Therefore, the ability of a collective's individuals to work with dysfunction is crucial in determining the collective's antifragility.

When coaching collectives, we focus on opportunities, strengths, weaknesses, and threats as they work with dysfunction.

Trust, conflict, and cohesion issues. This collective experienced an absence of trust and a fear of conflict, and involved individuals who were unwilling to be vulnerable within the collective and individuals who stifled constructive conflict and preserved artificial harmony. We worked together to explore working with conflict and cohesion.

Then, I suggested the collective focus on those opportunities, strengths, weaknesses, and threats that involved progressively more trust and conflict issues.

As I stressed the collective so as to encourage it to confront more trust and conflict issues, its members became more aware of their need for commitment, accountability, and results.

Commitment, accountability, and results issues. This collective experienced a lack of commitment, avoided accountability, and did not pay attention to results; it also involved individuals who had a lack of clarity and buy-in, hesitated to hold one another accountable, and put their individual needs above the collective's needs. We explored working with commitment, accountability, and ownership of results.

We first considered opportunities, strengths, weaknesses, and threats that could be addressed through minimal to no commitment, accountability, and results – which included almost nothing. Then, I coached the collective to focus on those opportunities, strengths, weaknesses, and threats that involved progressively more commitment, accountability, and results issues.

As I coached the collective to confront more commitment, accountability, and results issues, they became more aware of their performance. The collective began to recognize that getting past commitment, accountability, and results issues was crucial to exploring options and performing experiments together as well as to fostering redundancy and distributing power. The collective's members began to realize that a focus on commitment, accountability, and results could make them more dependent on one another.

These examples demonstrate that a collective where individuals work with dysfunction can focus on options, experiments, redundancy, and power. Therefore, such a collective is more antifragile.

CONFLICT

In *Introduction to Conflict Management,* Kenneth W. Thomas and Ralph H. Kilmann (2002) effectively explore working with conflict and using conflict-handling modes. While I only provide foundational background information regarding conflict, before exploring how this information relates to antifragility, I encourage you to explore Thomas and Kilmann's work for an even deeper understanding.

Background

Because antifragility requires us to be entrepreneurs who seek opportunities and thrive as well as being adventurers who seek experiences and evolve, a collective's ability to work with conflict is foundational for its dynamics, including its interaction with reality and experience of reality.

Conflict is at the core of groups coalescing. Groups naturally experience stress when working with conflict.

A conflict is a situation or condition concerning issues that people care about; such issues may appear incompatible with one another. Conflicts naturally emerge from people's differences and interdependence. A positive outcome, which involves high-quality decisions (D of OODA) and actions (A of OODA), can result from effectively working with conflict. A negative outcome, which involves poor-quality decisions and actions, can result from ineffectively working with conflict. A conflict is not mere aggression. A conflict may be addressed constructively with conflict-handling modes or destructively with aggression. Each conflict-handling mode is a general intention or choice in confronting and dealing with conflict in terms of two underlying dimensions: assertiveness and cooperativeness. These focus on the degree to which one individual tries to satisfy their own concerns (taking) and another individual's concerns (giving) respectively.

The **avoiding** conflict-handling mode involves sidestepping the conflict without satisfying either individual's concerns. This is commonly called a 'lose–lose' solution and involves both individuals withholding their time and energy from working with the conflict. While this conflict-handling mode may reduce stress and save time and energy, it could degrade the relationship and cause future delays.

A collective where individuals avoid conflict is a group that has not yet integrated all of its individuals.

The **competing** conflict-handling mode involves one individual satisfying their own concerns at the expense of satisfying the other individual's concerns. This is commonly called a 'win–lose' solution and involves both individuals investing some of their time and energy to work with the conflict issue but with the first individual taking more and giving less than the other individual. The first individual gains at the expense of the other individual. While this conflict-handling mode may involve asserting a position and lead to a quick victory, it could strain the relationship.

The **accommodating** conflict-handling mode involves one individual satisfying the other individual's concerns at the expense of satisfying their own concerns. This is commonly called a 'lose–win' solution and involves both individuals investing some of their time and energy to work with the conflict issue but with the first individual giving more and taking less than the other individual. The other individual gains at the expense of the first individual. While this conflict-handling mode may build the relationship and quickly end a conflict, it could sacrifice concerns.

The **compromising** conflict-handling mode involves one individual partially satisfying both their own concerns and the other individual's concerns at the expense of both individuals. This may be called either a 'win–lose' solution or a 'lose–win' solution and involves both individuals investing some of their time and energy to work with the conflict issue and both individuals taking, giving, and splitting the difference. Both individuals gain and lose. While this conflict-handling mode may maintain the relationship and foster pragmatism, it could lead to a suboptimal solution.

A collective where individuals compete, accommodate, and compromise fosters conditions in which individuals explore options and perform experiments together and become redundant and disturb power among themselves while working towards the collective's intentions. This process functions similarly to the storming and norming stages discussed in the Groups section of this chapter. However, because the individuals embrace a 'win–lose' perspective and try to address concerns with the mindset that there is a sense of limited value, they are more fragile.

The **collaborating** conflict-handling mode involves one individual completely satisfying both their own concerns and the other individual's concerns. This is commonly called a 'win–win' solution and involves both individuals investing their time and energy to work with the conflict issue and jointly creating more value than in the previous solutions. While this conflict-handling mode may strengthen the relationship and foster resolution and commitment, it could require time and energy and being vulnerable.

A collective where individuals collaborate fosters conditions in which individuals explore options and perform experiments together and become redundant and disturb power among themselves while working towards the collective's intentions. This process functions similarly to the performing stage, integrating the storming and norming stages, discussed in the Groups section of this chapter. However, because the individuals embrace a 'win–win' perspective and try to address concerns with the mindset that they can create more value, they are more antifragile. Furthermore, collaboration creates a dependency between individuals where the individuals depend on one another to collaborate together.

No one conflict-handling mode is inherently better or worse, but each is more or less effective in different situations based on the quality of decisions and actions, and the investment of time and energy.

A collective where individuals use avoiding, competing, accommodating, compromising, and collaborating will generally balance its ability to explore options and perform experiments together and be redundant and disturb power among its members. This can make the collective more antifragile.

Antifragility

How does conflict relate to antifragility?

A collective where individuals can work with conflict plays a crucial role in the individuals' ability to explore options, perform experiments, be redundant, and distribute power. Antifragility requires entrepreneurs who consider their options and experiment as well as adventurers who are independent, redundant, and share power. Entrepreneurs seek opportunities and thrive while adventurers seek experiences and evolve. Therefore, the ability of a collective's individuals to work with conflict is crucial in determining the collective's antifragility.

When coaching collectives, we focus on opportunities, strengths, weaknesses, and threats as they work with conflict.

Avoid conflict. This collective involved individuals withholding their time and energy when dealing with conflict, and involved individuals sidestepping conflict without satisfying concerns. We worked together to explore the tendency to avoid conflict.

As I stressed the collective so as to encourage it to confront more conflict, its members became more aware of their need for competing, accommodating, and compromising. The collective began to recognize that getting past avoiding conflict was crucial.

Compete, accommodate, or compromise. This collective involved individuals investing only some of their time and energy when dealing with conflict and individuals who believed that they could only claim limited value; it also involved individuals who tried to partially satisfy concerns. We worked together to explore the tendency to compete, accommodate, or compromise.

Then, I coached the collective to focus on those opportunities, strengths, weaknesses, and threats that involved progressively more competing, accommodating, and compromising.

As I stressed the collective so as to encourage it to confront more competing, accommodating, and compromising, its members became more aware of their need for collaboration.

Collaborate. This collective involved individuals investing their time and energy when dealing with conflict and believing that they could create more value; it also involved individuals who tried to completely satisfy concerns. We explored the tendency to collaborate.

First, we focused on those opportunities, strengths, weaknesses, and threats that could be addressed through collaboration. Then, I coached the collective to focus on those opportunities, strengths, weaknesses, and threats that involved progressively more collaboration.

As I coached the collective to use more collaboration, its members became more aware of their focus on any one conflict-handling mode and of the need to balance all conflict-handling modes. The collective began to recognize that using the collaborating conflict-handling mode was crucial to exploring options and performing experiments together as well as to fostering redundancy and distributing power. The collective's members began to realize that a focus on collaboration could make them more dependent on one another.

These examples demonstrate that a collective where individuals work with conflict can focus on options, experiments, redundancy, and power. Therefore, such a collective is more antifragile.

TEAMING

Here I have provided background information regarding teaming and how it relates to antifragility. But I encourage you to explore Amy C. Edmondson's book *Teaming* (2014) for an even deeper understanding.

Background

Because collectives must fluidly navigate and synchronize with one another, signal and trigger each other, and anchor or bind together and un-anchor or un-bind from each other based on common goals, teaming is foundational to their dynamics, including their interactions with reality and experiences of reality. And, because antifragility requires us to be entrepreneurs who seek opportunities and thrive as well as adventurers who seek experiences and evolve, teaming is foundational for antifragility and for being entrepreneurs.

Again, options and experiments are the 'currency' through which we seek opportunities as entrepreneurs, and independence and redundancy are the currency through which we seek experiences as adventurers. The more options and the more experiments, the more potential for opportunities, which power thriving. The more independence, redundancy, and distribution of power, the more potential for experiences, which power evolving.

Notice that functioning as a group, working with dysfunction, and working with conflict are foundational to teaming. With teaming, groups naturally experience stress when functioning as a group, working with dysfunction, and working with conflict.

While a collective is merely a group of individuals, a team is a collective of individuals in pursuit of a **common goal**. A team is a static entity. Teaming is a **dynamic activity**. Compared to interactions within communities, teaming involves **more short-lived and more temporary groups**. That is, teaming involves groups of fluid individuals who engage around more temporary focal points in a more short-lived or shorter-lived way.

Teaming involves a way of working (teaming), a way of leading (organizing to learn), and a way of operating (execution as learning). An enterprise is composed of a constellation of interconnected and flowing teams via teaming, which fosters more short-lived and more temporary groups, within a lattice that includes communities.

Teaming involves conversations; collaboration via cooperation and coordination of behaviours within the group; experimentation via an incremental and iterative approach to taking action (OODA) and learning from the results; and reflection via an incremental and iterative approach to observing (OODA) and learning from the results.

Teaming integrates conversations similarly to how Glaser (2013) describes conversations in *Conversational Intelligence*, relationships similarly to how Logan, King and, Fischer-Wright (2011) describe relationships in *Tribal Leadership*, and behaviours similarly to how Herrero (2008) describes behaviours in *Viral Change*. It integrates individual antifragility gained through conversations, relationships, and behaviours.

Organizing to learn involves leading by fostering a learning mindset, psychological safety, learning from failure, and collaboration with others outside the group. Fundamentally, this involves organizing to experiment with options.

Execution as learning involves operating through 'loose' cycles of diagnosing, designing, acting, and reflecting:

- **Diagnosing** involves assessing a situation for performance, threats, or opportunities. This is similar to observation in OODA.

- **Designing** involves developing an action plan to improve performance, consider alternatives for addressing threats, or consider experiments for seizing opportunities. This is similar to deciding in OODA.

- **Acting** involves enacting an action plan to learn about improving performance, testing alternatives, or performing experiments. This is similar to acting in OODA.

- **Reflecting** involves learning from outcomes and determining whether performance improved, whether using an alternative approach addressed threats, or whether experiments seized opportunities. This is similar to orientation in OODA.

Fundamentally, this involves experimenting with options. Diagnosing, designing, acting, and reflecting are not as separate or as linear as they may seem.

While teams must themselves evolve, teaming empowers the enterprise to seek opportunities and thrive. Teams focus on options and experiments, as collectives of entrepreneurs that power an antifragile enterprise.

When working with **teams**, identify the various individuals' goals. Organize the goals by grouping similar goals together and separating out differing goals, and ultimately identify various clusters of common goals, and consider these common goals in relation to the enterprise's goals, as discussed in Chapter 5. These focal points represent results (solutions, experiences, products, or services).

Form teams to create, discover, develop, and seize opportunities. Form teams to first address threats and second transform threats into opportunities. For strengths and weaknesses, focus on communities. Teaming is focused on seeking opportunities and thriving.

As teams are established, ensure they perform, work with dysfunction, and work with conflict. Those teams that don't perform to meet their goals or that don't work with dysfunction and conflict should be disbanded with their individuals joining other teams. The individuals will begin to recognize that teaming focuses on exploring options and performing experiments, and seeking opportunities and thriving.

Fundamentally, launch and disband teams around dynamic focal points that morph over time. Ensure team and enterprise hygiene and health, so that the teams and enterprise will be more agile and antifragile so as to adapt, survive, evolve, and thrive rather than be fragile or anti-agile. Perpetuating teams that demonstrably ought to be disbanded, simply because they exist, is unhealthy. Furthermore, excessive hygiene, beyond a certain point, causes more fragility than antifragility. Additionally, a team could be composed of sub-teams to further foster scale.

When working with **individuals and teams**, expose the individuals to various experiences that will make clear the reality that they are experiencing as quickly as possible, so as to preserve as much as possible of the individuals, collective, and enterprise; also raise their awareness of their performance as a team.

Expose the individuals to experiences that will stress or nudge them just enough to raise their awareness and not under-stress or over-stress the individuals. The stress must be acute rather than chronic and must be distributed over time so as to only harm the individuals to a manageable degree. The degree of stress must be such that the individuals gain from it, and the individuals must have sufficient time to recover from the harm and gain from the stress.

Using stress to foster teams and teaming can be a very delicate matter. This involves stressing individuals and the team and considering how the individuals stress each other as well as how the team stresses other collectives and is stressed by other collectives in the enterprise. While there is value to stressing individuals in a team and in the process of forming a team, the team's performance is crucial. Furthermore, when teams don't become healthy, disbanding them can be more art than science, and is more experimentation than anything else.

When working with teams, we need to consider **self-management**, **self-direction**, and **self-organization** as well as their **encapsulation**, **cohesion**, **coupling**, and **orchestration**. The 'richness' or complexity of an enterprise relates to how individuals and collectives orchestrate within the enterprise – that is, coordination across the enterprise.

Notice that, while teaming from an enterprise point of view focuses on exploring options and performing experiments and on seeking opportunities and thriving, communities focus on fostering redundancy and distributing power and on seeking experiences and evolving. Teaming and communities are complementary in integrating competing tensions between external dynamics and internal dynamics towards cultivating a healthy enterprise. The integration of teams and communities forms the scaffolding of an enterprise, the interlocking elements that form a network.

Antifragility

How does teaming foster antifragility?

A collective where individuals can team through teaming plays a crucial role in the individuals' ability to explore options, perform experiments, and seek opportunities and thrive. Antifragility requires entrepreneurs who consider their options and experiment as well as adventurers who are independent, redundant, and share power. Entrepreneurs seek opportunities and thrive while adventurers seek experiences and evolve. Teaming is essential for seeking opportunities from which to thrive. Therefore, the ability of a collective's individuals to team through teaming is crucial in determining the team's antifragility.

When coaching teams, we focus on opportunities, strengths, weaknesses, and threats by addressing teaming issues, organizing-to-learn issues, and execution-as-learning issues as well as exploring how to organize.

Teaming issues. This collective experienced issues with conversations, collaboration, experimentation, and reflection. We worked together to explore how these issues negatively impacted the collective.

Then, I coached the collective to focus on those opportunities, strengths, weaknesses, and threats that involved progressively more teaming issues.

As I stressed the collective so as to encourage it to confront teaming issues, they became more aware of their performance. The collective began to recognize that overcoming teaming issues was crucial to exploring options and performing experiments together.

Organizing-to-learn issues. This collective experienced issues with a learning mindset, psychological safety, learning from failure, and collaboration. We explored how these issues negatively impacted the collective.

Then, I stressed the collective so as to encourage it to focus on those opportunities, strengths, weaknesses, and threats that involved progressively more organizing-to-learn issues.

As I stressed the collective so as to encourage it to confront organizing-to-learn issues, its members became more aware that overcoming organizing-to-learn issues was crucial to exploring options and performing experiments together.

Execution-as-learning issues. This collective experienced issues with diagnosing, designing, acting, and reflecting. We explored how these issues negatively impacted the collective.

Then, I stressed the collective so as to encourage it to focus on those opportunities, strengths, weaknesses, and threats that involved progressively more execution-as-learning issues.

As I stressed the collective so as to encourage it to confront execution-as-learning issues, its members became more aware that overcoming execution-as-learning issues was crucial to exploring options and performing experiments together.

Exploring how to organize. I raised awareness of goals as more temporary focal points and teaming as a dynamic activity for forming more short-lived and more temporary groups.

We identified various goals among the group of individuals and explored how these related to the enterprise's goals and how these represented results (solutions, experiences, products, or services).

As we formed teams around these goals and then had to disband some teams and form other teams based on how goals changed, the individuals began to recognize that teaming focuses on exploring options and performing experiments, and on seeking opportunities and thriving.

These examples demonstrate that a collective where individuals team through teaming can explore options and perform experiments, and can seek opportunities and thrive. Therefore, such a team is more antifragile.

COMMUNITIES OF PRACTICE

In *Communities of Practice* (1999) and *Learning in Landscapes of Practice* (2014), Étienne Wenger explores communities. Here I explore how communities relate to antifragility. But, for an even deeper understanding, I encourage you to explore Étienne Wenger's work.

Background

Because collectives must fluidly navigate and synchronize with one another, signal and trigger each other, and anchor or bind together and un-anchor or un-bind from each other based on common passions, organizing as communities is foundational to their dynamics, including their interactions with reality and experiences of reality. And, because antifragility requires us to be entrepreneurs who seek opportunities and thrive as well as adventurers who seek experiences and evolve, communities are foundational for antifragility and for being adventurers.

Again, options and experiments are the 'currency' through which we seek opportunities as entrepreneurs and opportunities to thrive, and independence and re-dundancy are the currency through which we seek experiences as adventurers and opportunities to evolve.

Notice that functioning as a group, working with dysfunction, and working with conflict are foundational to organizing as communities. With communities, groups naturally experience stress when functioning as a group, working with dysfunction, and working with conflict.

While a collective is merely a group of individuals, a community is a collective of individuals in pursuit of a **common passion**. A community is a **dynamic entity**. Compared to interactions within teams via teaming, communities involve **more long-lived and more permanent groups**. That is, communities involve groups of fluid individuals that are more long-lived or longer-lived around more permanent focal points.

A community involves a domain, a community, and a practice. An enterprise is composed of a constellation of interconnected and flowing communities that foster more long-lived and more permanent groups, within a lattice that includes teams via teaming.

A domain involves a **joint enterprise**. A community focuses on a domain, the subject of the community. A community has an identity where membership implies a commitment to the domain and a shared competence that distinguishes members from non-members.

A community involves **mutual engagement**. A community involves community members who share experiences and learn from one another. A community has a sense of aliveness where members engage in activities and conversations and support each other.

A practice involves a **shared repertoire**. A community involves members who are practitioners, practising what they learn while continuing to expand their learning based in practice. A community develops a shared repertoire of resources that improves individual and collective performance.

A community spans organizational structure, both within organizational units and across organizational units. A community is not an organizational unit; the boundaries of a community are flexible while organizational units define an organization's structure. A community is not a team; the focus of a community is on knowledge rooted in practice and knowledge applied in practice while a team's focus is on tasks and a specific effort. A community is not a network; the focus of a community is on a subject while a network's focus is on relationships. Communities enable people to have collective responsibility and ownership in contributing to their individual and the enterprise's performance.

A community also has a natural cycle of birth, growth, and death. Birth involves a group of people who have the potential to become more connected, and, as they become more connected, they coalesce into a community. Growth involves the community maturing through active stewardship. And, ultimately, death involves the people in the community transforming and the community dissolving.

Communities form around real problems and solutions, are self-defined and self-managed, and are logistically supported and sponsored by the enterprise. A community is launched with a core group (sometimes called a 'nucleus') that organizes an initial series of value-adding activities. Ultimately, a community coordinator helps to shepherd the community to foster a win–win solution for each individual, the community, and the enterprise.

While communities must themselves evolve, communities empower the enterprise to seek experiences and evolve. As collectives of adventurers that power an antifragile enterprise, communities focus on redundancy and distributing power.

When working with **communities**, identify the various individuals' passions. Organize the passions by grouping similar passions together and separating differing passions, and ultimately identify various clusters of common passions. These focal points represent capabilities and competencies needed to realize results (or solutions, experiences, products, or services).

Form communities to maximize strengths. Form communities to first minimize weaknesses and second transform weaknesses into strengths. For opportunities and threats, focus on teaming. Communities are focused on seeking experiences and evolving.

As communities are established, ensure they perform, work with dysfunction, and work with conflict. Those communities that don't perform to grow their passions or that don't work with dysfunction and conflict should be disbanded with their individuals joining other communities. The individuals will begin to recognize that communities focus on fostering redundancy and distributing power, and seeking experiences and evolving.

Fundamentally, launch and disband communities around dynamic focal points that morph over time. Ensure community and enterprise hygiene and health, so that the communities and enterprise will be more agile and antifragile so as to adapt, survive, evolve, and thrive rather than be fragile or anti-agile. Perpetuating communities that demonstrably ought to be disbanded, simply because they exist, is unhealthy. Furthermore, excessive hygiene, beyond a certain point, causes more fragility than antifragility. Additionally, a community could be composed of sub-communities or committees to further foster scale.

When working with **individuals and communities**, expose the individuals to various experiences that will make clear the reality that they are experiencing as quickly as possible, so as to preserve as much as possible of the individuals, collective, and enterprise; also raise their awareness of their performance as a community.

Expose the individuals to experiences that will stress or nudge them just enough to raise their awareness and not under-stress or over-stress the individuals. The stress must be acute rather than chronic and must be distributed over time so as to only harm the individuals to a manageable degree. The degree of stress must be such that the individuals gain from it, and the individuals must have sufficient time to recover from the harm and gain from the stress.

Using stress to foster communities and organizing communities can be a very delicate matter. This involves stressing individuals and the community, and considering how the individuals stress each other as well as how the community stresses other collectives and is stressed by other collectives in the enterprise. While there is value to stressing individuals in a community and to encouraging them to form a community, the community's performance is crucial. Furthermore, when communities don't become healthy, disbanding them can be more art than science, and is more experimentation than anything else.

Notice that, while communities from an enterprise point of view focus on fostering redundancy and distributing power and on seeking experiences and evolving, teaming focuses on exploring options and performing experiments and on seeking opportunities and thriving. Communities and teaming are complementary in integrating competing tensions between internal dynamics and external dynamics towards cultivating a healthy enterprise. The integration of communities and teams forms the scaffolding of an enterprise, the interlocking elements that form a network.

Antifragility

How do communities foster antifragility?

A collective where individuals can organize as a community plays a crucial role in the individuals' ability to be redundant, distribute power, be independent, and seek experiences and evolve. Antifragility requires entrepreneurs who consider their options and experiment as well as adventurers who are independent, redundant, and share power. Entrepreneurs seek opportunities and thrive while adventurers seek experiences and evolve. Communities are essential for seeking experiences from which to evolve. Therefore, the ability of a collective's individuals to organize as a community is crucial in determining the community's antifragility.

When coaching communities, we focus on opportunities, strengths, weaknesses, and threats by addressing community issues as well as exploring how to organize.

Community issues. This collective experienced issues with the subject of the community, engagement among community members, and members practising what they learn while continuing to expand their learning based in practice. We worked together to explore how these issues negatively impacted the collective.

Then, I coached the collective to focus on those opportunities, strengths, weaknesses, and threats that involved progressively more community issues.

As I stressed the collective so as to encourage it to confront community issues, its members became more aware of their performance. They began to recognize that overcoming community issues was crucial to fostering redundancy and distributing power.

Exploring how to organize. I raised awareness of passions as more permanent focal points and communities as dynamic entities for forming more long-lived and more permanent groups.

We identified various passions among the group of individuals and explored how these represented capabilities and competencies needed to realize results (solutions, experiences, products, or services).

As we formed communities around these passions and then had to disband some communities and form other communities based on how passions changed, the individuals began to recognize that communities focus on fostering redundancy and distributing power, and on seeking experiences.

These examples demonstrate that a collective where individuals organize as a community can foster redundancy and distribute power, and can seek experiences and evolve. Therefore, such a community is more antifragile.

ACHIEVING COLLECTIVE ANTIFRAGILITY

To achieve greater antifragility, a collective must interact with reality and experience reality through teaming and communities. Its members must embrace reality and thrive in it. They must ensure they are evolving based on their strengths, weaknesses, opportunities, and threats as well as observations, orientation, decisions, and actions. As collectives, how we work as groups, work with dysfunction, and work with conflict exemplify our collective identity and our antifragility.

To achieve greater antifragility, collectives navigate and synchronize with one another and signal and trigger each other via teaming and organizing as communities. A collective's flow across the enterprise determines its antifragility.

A team is a collective of individuals in pursuit of a common goal, a more short-lived and more temporary group. A team is a static entity. Teaming is a dynamic activity. That is, teaming involves short-lived groups of fluid individuals organized around temporary focal points.

A community is a collective of individuals in pursuit of a common passion, a more long-lived and more permanent group. A community is a dynamic entity. That is, communities involve long-lived groups of fluid individuals organized around more permanent focal points.

Antifragility requires us to be entrepreneurs and adventurers. As entrepreneurs, we consider our options and experiment to seek opportunities and thrive. As adventurers, we individually don't specialize and are very independent in seeking experiences and evolving. As adventurers, we collectively become redundant and share power to seek experiences and evolve.

Herein is a summary of the sections in this chapter.

- **Groups, dysfunctions, and conflict:** A collective where individuals work as a group, work with dysfunction, and work with conflict can explore options and perform experiments together as well as foster redundancy and distribute power, but individuals are dependent on one another.

- **Teaming:** A collective where individuals team through teaming can explore options and perform experiments, and seek opportunities and thrive.

- **Communities:** A collective where individuals organize as a community can foster redundancy and distribute power, and seek experiences and evolve.

Functioning as a group, working with dysfunction, and working with conflict while teaming or organizing as a community over time powers a collective to achieve greater antifragility.

Consider a collective that is developing as a team or community, working with dysfunction, and working with conflict. Coaching this collective, I recognized and appreciated the 'mystery' of their collectivity and shared identity. I raised awareness of the collective's functioning, working with dysfunction, and working with conflict. When some of the collective's initiatives were challenged, I observed and became increasingly aware of the collective's strengths, weaknesses, opportunities, and threats. We worked together to explore the initiatives, challenges, and situations as well as the collective's strengths, weaknesses, opportunities, and threats. Working with our awareness, first, we focused on those strengths, weaknesses, opportunities, and threats that could be addressed with minimal stress while accomplishing what needed to be achieved. Furthermore, working with our awareness, we then focused on creating and discovering opportunities. And, working with our awareness, then, I coached the collective to focus on those strengths, weaknesses, opportunities, and threats that involved progressively more stress while accomplishing what needed to be achieved. As I stressed the collective, the collective became more aware of itself and everything around it. The collective began to become more antifragile.

In all of the cases throughout this chapter, stress is related to the collective's ability to work as a group, ability to work with dysfunction, ability to work with conflict, ability to team through teaming, and ability to organize as communities; ultimately, this stress helps the collective to:

- create, discover, develop, and seize opportunities
- address threats and transform them into opportunities
- maximize and develop strengths
- minimize weaknesses and transform them into strengths
- adjust and develop the collective's observations, orientation, decisions, and actions.

While Tuckman (1965), Lencioni (2002), Thomas and Kilmann (2002), Edmondson (2014), Wenger (1999), and Wenger (2014) respectively focus on a collective's ability to work as a group, work with dysfunction, work with conflict, team through teaming, and organize as communities, there are other works that may be of value. However, I have found these to be demonstrably beneficial in fostering antifragility in practice.

CHAPTER 4

ENTERPRISE ANTI-FRAGILITY

Thischapter explores how an enterprise operationalizes antifragility through adapting, surviving, evolving, and thriving independently at every level (individual, collective, and enterprise) and interdependently across all levels.

How does an enterprise **interact with reality** and **experience reality**?

Our interactions with reality and experiences of reality as an enterprise, composed of individuals and collectives, are rooted in our adapting, surviving, evolving, and thriving, both internally among individuals and collectives and externally within the context or environment of the enterprise. Our adapting, surviving, evolving, and thriving independently at every level – individual, collective, and enterprise – and interdependently across all levels exemplify our enterprise's identity and our antifragility.

ENTERPRISE ANTIFRAGILITY

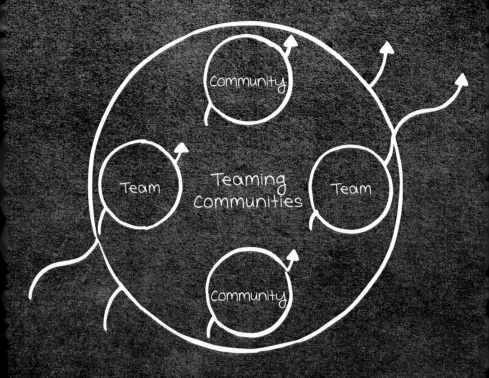

How does an enterprise **embrace reality** and thrive as well as **ensure its aliveness** and evolve? The constituents of an enterprise embrace reality like entrepreneurs who seek opportunities from which to thrive, and they ensure their aliveness like adventurers who seek experiences from which to evolve. An enterprise is composed of a lattice of teams and communities.

Teaming involves short-lived and temporary groups. That is, teaming involves short-lived groups of fluid individuals organized around temporary focal points. An enterprise is composed of a constellation of interconnected and flowing teams via teaming.

Communities involve more long-lived and more permanent groups. That is, communities involve more long-lived groups of fluid individuals organized around more permanent focal points. An enterprise is composed of a constellation of interconnected and flowing communities.

How do an **enterprise's strengths, weaknesses, opportunities, and threats** relate to antifragility? An enterprise might approach a situation by appraising its strengths and weaknesses from an internal viewpoint through communities and by appraising its opportunities and threats from an external viewpoint through teams.

How do an **enterprise's observations, orientation, decisions, and actions** relate to antifragility? An enterprise might observe, orient, decide, and act to adapt and survive as well as evolve and thrive through teams and communities.

ADAPTIVE CYCLES

Here I have provided background information regarding adaptive cycles and how they relate to antifragility. For more information, please explore Crawford Stanley Holling's (2001) work, which explores adapting, surviving, evolving, and thriving independently at every level.

Background

Because individuals, collectives, and enterprises must adapt, survive, evolve, and thrive, adaptive cycles are foundational to their dynamics, including their interactions with reality and experiences of reality. And, because antifragility requires being entrepreneurs who seek opportunities and thrive as well as being adventurers who seek experiences and evolve, adaptive cycles are foundational for antifragility, independently at every level.

Again, options and experiments are the 'currency' through which we seek opportunities as entrepreneurs, and independence and redundancy are the currency through which we seek experiences as adventurers. The more options and the more experiments, the more potential for opportunities, which power thriving. The more independence and being redundant and distributing power, the more potential for experiences, which power evolving.

Notice that individual antifragility – as described in Chapter 2, where I discuss how mindsets, questions, and leadership are foundational to conversations, relationships, and behaviours – is foundational to collective antifragility – as described in Chapter 3, where I discuss how functioning as a group, working with dysfunction, and working with conflict are foundational to teaming and organizing as communities. Collective antifragility is also foundational to enterprise antifragility.

The adaptive cycle describes the transformational cycle (or lifecycle) of an entity (individual, collective, or enterprise) and its constituents or aspects in terms of three properties: potential, connectedness, and adaptive capacity.

ADAPTIVE CYCLE

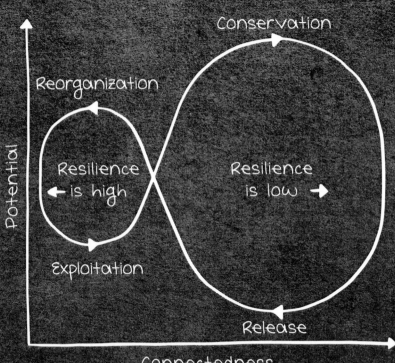

The notion of an entity is used to generalize how we work with the concepts of adaptation and evolution as they relate to an individual, a collective, and an enterprise:

- an entity may be an individual and the individual's aspects include conversations, relationships, behaviours, and competencies
- an entity may be a collective and the collective's constituents include the individuals that compose the collective
- an entity may be an enterprise and the enterprise's constituents include the individuals and collectives that compose the enterprise.

An entity forms because its constituents or aspects have spatial and temporal proximity – that is, are in a proximate space and share a similar speed in terms of operating at a similar pace.

The potential property of an entity is determined by the value that the entity's aspects contribute to the entity's future options. The connectedness property of an entity is determined by the **degree of integration** (or internal integration) between the entity's aspects, which determines the degree the entity can control its destiny rather than be at the whims of external variability. The adaptive capacity property of an entity is determined by the **degree of adaptability** (or external adaptation) of the entity's aspects in relation to the entity's context or environment, which determines how vulnerable the entity is to unexpected disturbances.

The notions of constituents or aspects, potential, connectedness, and adaptive capacity are used to generalize how we (whether as individuals, collectives, or enterprises) work with the concepts of adapting, surviving, evolving, and thriving, both internally through integration and externally through adaptability.

Notice that the degree of internal integration focuses on evolving and the degree of external adaptation focuses on adapting. Enterprises naturally experience stress when adapting and evolving.

The adaptive cycle of an entity alternates between a front-loop, which includes the exploitation and conservation phases, and a back-loop, which includes the release and reorganization phases. The front-loop and back-loop continuously revitalize the entity.

The **front-loop** focuses on **growth and stability**. It occurs over a comparatively long and slow period of time involving production and accumulation, and progresses from **exploitation** (growth) to **conservation** (maturation); during this process, potential and connectedness increase, and things become progressively more **predictable**. Similarly, adaptive capacity decreases as an entity transitions from growth to maturation. Ultimately, the entity becomes rigid, over-connected, and maladaptive and then abruptly collapses, at which point its potential drops and the adaptive cycle transitions into the back-loop. The front-loop is where the entity develops.

The **back-loop** focuses on **change and variety**. It occurs over a comparatively short and fast period of time involving invention, experimentation and innovation, and re-assortment (of aspects), and progresses from **release** (death) to **reorganization** (renewal); during this process of Joseph Alois Schumpeter's creative destruction (2016), potential increases and connectedness decreases, and things are inherently **unpredictable** and highly uncertain. Similarly, adaptive capacity increases as an entity transitions from death to renewal. Ultimately, the entity is reborn and the adaptive cycle transitions into the front-loop. The back-loop is where opportunity is created (or nucleated) via release and reorganization.

Notice that growth and maturation foster predictability, and release and reorganization occurs because of unpredictability. The notions of death and renewal emphasize how an individual, a collective, and an enterprise achieve independence, the ability to explore options and perform experiments, and the ability to foster redundancy and distribute power. Essentially, it shows how everything adapts, survives, evolves, and thrives independently at every level.

An enterprise experiences an adaptive cycle as individuals and collectives grow, mature, release, and reorganize as an enterprise. An enterprise becomes more antifragile when it grows and matures some individuals and collectives as well as releases and reorganizes other individuals and collectives based on their independence, ability to explore options and perform experiments, and ability to foster redundancy and distribute power. In this way, the enterprise experiences very natural stress.

A collective experiences an adaptive cycle as the group forms, storms, norms, performs through its innovativeness, and adjourns as a team. A team becomes more antifragile when it grows and matures some individuals as well as releases and reorganizes other individuals based on their independence and ability to explore options and perform experiments. In this way, the team experiences very natural stress.

A collective experiences an adaptive cycle as the group is born, grows through its innovativeness, and dies as a community. A community becomes more antifragile when it grows and matures some individuals as well as releases and reorganizes other individuals based on their independence and ability to foster redundancy and distribute power. In this way, the community experiences very natural stress.

Individuals experience an adaptive cycle as they grow, mature, release, and reorganize their conversations, relationships, behaviours, and competencies to foster their creativity. Individuals become more antifragile when they grow and mature (sometimes known as cultivating) some conversations, relationships, behaviours, and competencies as well as release and reorganize (sometimes known as reshaping). This is based on their own independence, ability to explore options and perform experiments, and ability to foster redundancy and distribute power. Individuals can grow and mature their competencies by learning and honing them as well as releasing and reorganizing their competencies by unlearning and re-learning. In this way, individuals experience very natural stress.

Individuals and collectives must stress other individuals and collectives, but only enough to foster healthy dynamics rather than under-stress or over-stress – healthy dynamics foster the ability to adapt, survive, evolve, and thrive. An enterprise must stress its collectives and individuals based on the enterprise's context, but only enough to foster healthy dynamics rather than under-stress or over-stress – healthy dynamics foster the ability to adapt, survive, evolve, and thrive. The notion of the 'right' degree of stress is crucial and is discovered empirically through experimentation more than through anything else. This is a dance between embracing reality and ensuring aliveness where disorder or stress is at the intersection.

Antifragility

How do adaptive cycles foster antifragility?

An antifragile enterprise is one where the individuals and collectives that constitute the enterprise grow, mature, release, and reorganize based on their independence, ability to explore options and perform experiments, and ability to foster redundancy and distribute power. Adaptive cycles are essential for adapting, surviving, evolving, and thriving independently at every level.

When coaching enterprises, collectives, and individuals, we focus on working with opportunities, strengths, weaknesses, and threats by considering their cycles.

Enterprise cycle. This enterprise experienced great success but also significant challenges and obstacles as well as problematic circumstances. I raised awareness that adapting involves growing and maturing and evolving involves releasing and reorganizing; such changes may be induced by stress and can be used to foster healthy hygiene and success.

We identified individuals and collectives that contributed to and that detracted from the enterprise's performance. For those that contributed, we explored how best to help them evolve and thrive. For those that detracted, we explored how best to help them reorganize so that they didn't negatively impact other individuals, collectives, or the enterprise.

As I coached the individuals and collectives, the individuals and collectives became more aware of their contributions. The enterprise began to recognize that it must work with individuals and collectives that are more independent, that explore options and perform experiments, and that foster redundancy and distribute power. The enterprise began to reorganize individuals and collectives that were more dependent, that didn't explore options and perform experiments, and that didn't foster redundancy and distribute power. This ensured the enterprise's hygiene and health.

Team cycle. This team experienced great success but also significant challenges. I emphasized goals, teaming, and more temporary teams.

Focusing on people who contributed to and who detracted from the team's performance, we explored how best to help the contributors to evolve and thrive.

As I coached each person and the team as a whole, each person and the whole team became more aware of their contributions. The team began to recognize that it must work with individuals who are more independent and explore options and perform experiments.

Community cycle. This community experienced great success but also problematic circumstances. I emphasized passions and more long-lived communities.

Focusing on people who detracted from and who contributed to the community's performance, we worked with those who detracted so that they reorganized and didn't negatively impact other individuals, collectives, or the enterprise.

As I coached each person and the community as a whole, people and the whole community became more aware of their contributions. The community began to reorganize individuals who were more dependent and didn't foster redundancy and distribute power.

Individual cycle. This individual experienced great success but also opportunities for becoming more antifragile.

We identified conversations, relationships, and behaviours that contributed to and that detracted from their performance. For those that contributed, we explored how best to cultivate them. For those that detracted, we explored how best to reshape them.

Additionally, we explored their competencies. For those that contributed to their success and to possible future success, we explored how best to cultivate them. We then explored other possible competencies.

As a result, they became more aware of their contributions. They began to recognize that they must cultivate healthy conversations, relationships, and behaviours that foster their independence, their ability to explore options and perform experiments, and their ability to foster redundancy and distribute power. They also began to recognize that they must reshape unhealthy conversations, relationships, and behaviours that foster more dependence, an inability to explore options and perform experiments, and an inability to foster redundancy and distribute power so that they didn't negatively impact other conversations, relationships, and behaviours.

Additionally, they became more aware of their competencies. They began to recognize that they could not rely on their existing competencies but had to creatively learn some things and unlearn other things.

These examples demonstrate how adaptive cycles allow individuals, teams, communities, and enterprises to adapt, survive, evolve, and thrive independently at every level.

PANARCHY

In *Panarchy* (2001), Crawford Stanley Holling explores adapting, surviving, evolving, and thriving interdependently across all levels via panarchies. While I provide background information regarding panarchies and how they relate to antifragility, I encourage you to explore Holling's work for an even deeper understanding.

Background

Because individuals, collectives, and enterprises must adapt, survive, evolve, and thrive, panarchies are foundational to their dynamics, including their interactions with reality and experiences of reality. And, because antifragility requires us to be entrepreneurs who seek opportunities and thrive as well as adventurers who seek experiences and evolve, panarchies are foundational for antifragility, interdependently across all levels.

Again, options and experiments are the 'currency' through which we seek opportunities as entrepreneurs and opportunities to thrive; independence and redundancy are the currency through which we seek experiences as adventurers and opportunities to evolve.

Again, individual antifragility (as described in Chapter 2) is foundational to collective antifragility (as described in Chapter 3), which is also foundational to enterprise antifragility.

The concept of panarchy describes the hierarchical nature of an entity (individual, collective, and enterprise) as a nested set of adaptive cycles.

As each level (adaptive cycle) operates at its own pace, it is protected from above by a slower and larger adaptive cycle and invigorated from below by a faster and smaller adaptive cycle. The slower and larger adaptive cycle provides stability for the faster and smaller adaptive cycle, and the faster and smaller adaptive cycle generates innovations with experiments for the slower and larger adaptive cycle. The faster and smaller adaptive cycle continuously revitalizes the slower and larger adaptive cycle.

Notice the tension between stability or protection and invigoration or innovation; this is very natural stress.

At one level, when an entity enters its **release** phase, the collapse may cascade to the next slower and larger level by triggering a crisis, a cross-scale interaction. This is known as a **revolt** and involves the faster and smaller adaptive cycle **overwhelming** the slower and larger adaptive cycle. A revolt may further cascade to the next-larger and next-slower level.

At one level, when an entity enters its **reorganization** phase, the next-larger and next-slower level strongly influences the reorganization, a cross-scale interaction. This is known as a **remember** and involves the slower and larger adaptive cycle **constraining** the faster and smaller adaptive cycle.

Notice the tension between constraining and overwhelming; this is very natural stress.

The connection between larger and smaller levels is where **persistence** is created via remembers, and the connection between smaller and larger levels is where **evolve-ability** is created via revolts.

The notion of evolve-ability or revolts through experiments and the notion of persistence or remembers through stability emphasize how an individual, collective, and enterprise achieve independence, the ability to explore options and perform experiments, and the ability to foster redundancy and distribute power as individuals are fluid and collectives flow. Panarchies are the essence of antifragility relative to individuals' fluidity across collectives and collectives' flow across an enterprise. They are essential to how everything adapts, survives, evolves, and thrives interdependently across all levels.

An enterprise must cycle or operate slower than the individuals and collectives that make up the enterprise. Thus, the enterprise provides stability and persistence for the individuals and collectives. When an enterprise provides the 'right' degree of stability and stress, it becomes more antifragile and makes the individuals and collectives more antifragile by fostering their independence, their ability to explore options and perform experiments, and their ability to foster redundancy and distribute power. An enterprise should not coddle the individuals and collectives that make up the enterprise. Additionally, coddling makes the individuals, collectives, and enterprise more fragile.

A collective must cycle or operate faster than the enterprise to which it belongs. Thus, the collective invigorates and provides evolve-ability to the enterprise. When a collective invigorates the enterprise and other collectives and individuals with the 'right' degree of stress, it becomes more antifragile and makes the enterprise and other collectives and individuals more antifragile by being more independent, exploring options and performing experiments, and fostering redundancy and distributing power. A collective should not coddle the other collectives and individuals that make up the enterprise. Additionally, coddling makes the collective and the other collectives and individuals more fragile.

A collective must cycle or operate slower than the individuals that make up the collective. Thus, the collective provides stability and persistence for the individuals. When a collective provides the 'right' degree of stability and stress, it becomes more antifragile and makes the individuals more antifragile by fostering their independence, their ability to explore options and perform experiments, and their ability to foster redundancy and distribute power. A collective should not coddle the individuals that make up the collective. Additionally, coddling makes the collective and the individuals more fragile.

Individuals must cycle or operate faster than the collectives and enterprise to which they belong. Thus, individuals invigorate and provide evolve-ability to the collectives and the enterprise. When individuals invigorate the collectives and enterprise and other individuals with the 'right' degree of stress, they become more antifragile and make the collectives and enterprise and other individuals more antifragile by being independent, exploring options and performing experiments, and fostering redundancy and distributing power. An individual should not coddle the other individuals and collectives that make up the enterprise. Additionally, coddling makes the individual and the other individuals and collectives more fragile.

Individuals must stress their collectives and collectives must stress their enterprise, but only enough to foster healthy dynamics rather than under-stress or over-stress – healthy dynamics foster invigoration from the bottom up. An enterprise must stress its collectives and the collectives must stress their individuals, but only enough to foster healthy dynamics rather than under-stress or over-stress – healthy dynamics foster stability from the top down without negatively impacting invigoration from the bottom up. And similarly, individuals and collectives must stress other individuals and collectives, as discussed earlier in this chapter. The notion of the 'right' degree of stability, invigoration, and stress is crucial and is discovered empirically through experimentation more than through anything else. This is a dance between embracing reality and ensuring aliveness where disorder or stress is at the intersection.

Antifragility

How do panarchies foster antifragility?

An antifragile enterprise is one where the individuals and collectives that constitute the enterprise grow, mature, release, and reorganize based on their independence, ability to explore options and perform experiments, and ability to foster redundancy and distribute power. Panarchies are essential for adapting, surviving, evolving, and thriving interdependently across all levels.

When coaching enterprises, collectives, and individuals, we focus on working with opportunities, strengths, weaknesses, and threats by considering their interactions, stability, and innovativeness.

Enterprise interactions. This enterprise was exploring how to provide enough stability with the 'right' degree of stress for its individuals and collectives (teams and communities) so that they could perform and the enterprise could adapt, evolve, survive, and thrive.

We identified individuals and collectives who contributed to and who detracted from the enterprise's performance. For those who contributed, we explored how best to provide them with enough stability, but not so much as to inhibit innovation. For those who detracted, we explored how best to help them reorganize so that they didn't negatively impact other individuals, collectives, or the enterprise.

As I worked with the individuals and collectives, the individuals and collectives became more aware of their contributions and performance. The enterprise began to recognize that it must provide enough stability to the individuals and collectives who were more independent; explore options and perform experiments; foster redundancy and distribute power; and reorganize individuals and collectives who were more dependent, didn't explore options and perform experiments, and didn't foster redundancy and distribute power.

Team innovation. This team was exploring how to contribute to the enterprise to which it belonged.

Focusing on performance, we identified options and experiments that might generate innovation, but not so much as to over-stress the enterprise. First, we focused on those that could be achieved without too much stress.

Then, I coached the team to focus on those that involved progressively more stress.

As I coached the team and its members, the team and everyone became more aware of the need to consider their contributions and performance. The team began to recognize that it must be more independent, explore options, and perform experiments to contribute to the enterprise.

Community innovation. This community was exploring how to contribute to the enterprise to which it belonged.

With a focus on contribution, we explored ways of fostering redundancy and distributing power that might generate innovation, but not so much as to over-stress the enterprise. First, we focused on what could be achieved without too much stress. Then, we focused on what involved progressively more stress.

As I coached the community and its members, the community and everyone became more aware of their contributions and performance, and of the fact that they must foster redundancy and distribute power to contribute.

Team stability. This team was exploring how to provide enough stability with the 'right' degree of stress for the individuals on the team so that they could perform.

We considered individuals who contributed to their team's performance. We explored how best to provide additional stability to those who contributed and performed sufficiently, but not so much stability as to inhibit innovation.

The team members became more aware of their contributions and performance. The team began to recognize that it must provide enough stability to those who contributed.

Community stability. This community was exploring how to provide enough stability with the 'right' degree of stress for the individuals in the community so that they could perform.

We identified individuals who contributed to their community's performance. For those who did not, we explored how best to help them reorganize so that they didn't negatively impact others.

The individuals became more aware of their contributions and performance. The community began to recognize that it must reorganize those who didn't contribute.

Individual innovation. This individual was exploring how to contribute to the collectives and enterprise to which they belonged.

We identified options and experiments as well as ways of fostering redundancy and distributing power that might contribute to their performance by generating innovation, but not so much as to over-stress the collectives and enterprise to which the individual belonged. First, we focused on what could be achieved without too much stress. Then, we focused on what could be achieved with progressively more stress.

As I coached the individual, they became more aware of their contributions and performance. They began to recognize that they must be more independent, explore options, perform experiments, foster redundancy, and distribute power in order to contribute to the collectives and enterprise to which they belonged.

These examples demonstrate how panarchies integrate individuals, teams, communities, and the enterprise so everything can adapt, survive, evolve, and thrive interdependently across all levels.

ACHIEVING ENTERPRISE ANTIFRAGILITY

To achieve greater antifragility, an enterprise must interact with reality and experience reality through adapting, surviving, evolving, and thriving. It must embrace reality and thrive in it as well as ensure its aliveness and evolve based on its strengths, weaknesses, opportunities, and threats and its observations, orientation, decisions, and actions. Our adapting, surviving, evolving, and thriving independently at every level and interdependently across all levels exemplify our enterprise's identity and our antifragility.

As stakeholders (individuals and collectives) form an enterprise within an ecosystem, the dynamics among stakeholders and the evolution of the enterprise within its ecosystem determine the antifragility of the enterprise. The dynamics of how fluid an individual is, how flowing individuals are together as collectives, and how individuals and collectives work together dynamically as an enterprise determine the antifragility of the enterprise.

Antifragility requires us to be entrepreneurs and adventurers. As entrepreneurs, we consider our options and experiment to seek opportunities and thrive. As adventurers, we individually don't specialize and are very independent so as to seek experiences and evolve. As adventurers, we collectively become redundant and share power to seek experiences and evolve.

Herein is a summary of the concepts in this chapter.

- **Enterprise cycle:** An enterprise where individuals and collectives grow, mature, release, and reorganize based on their independence, ability to explore options and perform experiments, and ability to foster redundancy and distribute power is more antifragile.
- **Collective (team) cycle:** A collective where individuals team through teaming as they grow (storm and norm) and mature (perform) then release (adjourn) and reorganize (form) based on the individuals' independence and ability to explore options and perform experiments is more antifragile.
- **Collective (community) cycle:** A collective where individuals organize as a community as they grow and mature then release (die) and reorganize (form) based on the individuals' independence and ability to foster redundancy and distribute power is more antifragile.
- **Individual cycle:** An individual who can grow, mature, release, and reorganize their various conversations, relationships, behaviours, and competencies based on their independence, ability to explore options and perform experiments, and ability to foster redundancy and distribute power is more antifragile.
- **Enterprise interactions:** An enterprise that fosters the 'right' degree of stability and stress for those individuals and collectives that constitute the enterprise based on their independence, ability to explore options and perform experiments,

and ability to foster redundancy and distribute power is more antifragile.

- **Collective (team) interactions for innovation:** A collective (where individuals team through teaming) that fosters the 'right' degree of invigoration and stress on the enterprise to which it belongs (as well as other collectives and individuals) based on the individuals' independence and ability to explore options and perform experiments fosters enterprise antifragility.

- **Collective (community) interactions for innovation:** A collective (where individuals organize as a community) that fosters the 'right' degree of invigoration and stress on the enterprise to which it belongs (as well as other collectives and individuals) based on the individuals' independence and ability to foster redundancy and distribute power fosters enterprise antifragility.

- **Collective (team) interactions for stability:** A collective (where individuals team through teaming) that fosters the 'right' degree of stability and stress for those individuals based on their independence and ability to explore options and perform experiments is more antifragile.

- **Collective (community) interactions for stability:** A collective (where individuals organize as a community) that fosters the 'right' degree of stability and stress for those individuals based on their independence and ability to foster redundancy and distribute power is more antifragile.

- **Individual interactions:** Individuals who can foster the 'right' degree of invigoration and stress on the collectives and enterprise to which they belong (as well as on other individuals) based on their independence, ability to explore options and perform experiments, and ability to foster redundancy and distribute power fosters collective and enterprise antifragility.

Adapting, surviving, evolving, and thriving independently at every level and interdependently across all levels over time powers an enterprise to achieve greater antifragility.

Consider an enterprise that is adapting, surviving, evolving, and thriving. Coaching this enterprise, I recognized and appreciated the 'mystery' of the many individuals, collectives, and enterprise as a whole. I raised awareness of the enterprise's functioning and ability to adapt, survive, evolve, and thrive. When some of the enterprise's initiatives were challenged, I observed and became increasingly aware of the enterprise's strengths, weaknesses, opportunities, and threats. We worked together to explore the initiatives, challenges, and situations as well as the enterprise's strengths, weaknesses, opportunities, and threats. Working with our awareness, first, we focused on those strengths, weaknesses, opportunities, and threats that could be addressed with minimal stress while accomplishing what needed to be achieved. Furthermore, working with our awareness, we then focused on creating and discovering opportunities. And then, working with our awareness, I coached the enterprise to focus on those strengths, weaknesses, opportunities, and threats that involved progressively more stress while accomplishing what needed to be achieved. As I stressed the enterprise, the enterprise became more aware of itself and everything around it. The enterprise began to become more antifragile.

In all of the cases throughout this chapter, stress is related to an enterprise adapting, surviving, evolving, and thriving independently at every level and interdependently across all levels; ultimately it helps the enterprise to:

- create, discover, develop, and seize opportunities
- address threats and transform them into opportunities
- maximize and develop strengths
- minimize weaknesses and transform them into strengths
- adjust and develop the enterprise's observations, orientation, decisions, and actions.

While Holling's (2001) *Panarchy* focuses on adapting, surviving, evolving, and thriving independently at every level and interdependently across all levels, there are other works that may be of value. However, I have found this to be demonstrably beneficial in fostering antifragility in practice.

CHAPTER 5

ACHIEVING GREATER ANTI-FRAGILITY

Thⁱs chapter offers an actionable roadmap for how an enterprise can achieve greater antifragility through designing and creating itself and evolving and thriving.

As stakeholders (individuals and collectives) form an enterprise within an ecosystem, the dynamics among the stakeholders and the evolution of the enterprise within its ecosystem determine the antifragility of the enterprise. The dynamics of how fluid an individual is, how flowing individuals are together as collectives, and how individuals and collectives work together dynamically as an enterprise determine the antifragility of the enterprise.

ANTIFRAGILE ENTERPRISE

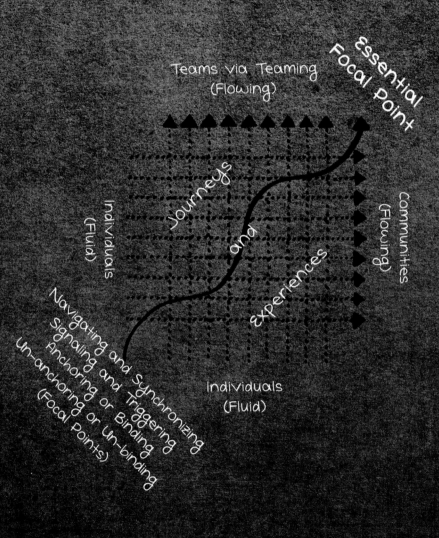

As we explored in Chapter 2, individuals navigate and synchronize with one another and signal and trigger each other via their dynamics, and an individual's fluidity across collectives and the enterprise determines the individual's antifragility.

As we explored in Chapter 3, collectives navigate and synchronize with one another and signal and trigger each other via their dynamics, and a collective's flow across an enterprise determines the collective's antifragility.

A **team** is a static, more short-lived, and more temporary collective formed around a more temporary and dynamic focal point, in pursuit of a common goal. Teaming is a dynamic activity that takes place when working with teams.

A **community** is a dynamic, more long-lived, and more permanent collective formed around a more permanent and dynamic focal point, in pursuit of a common passion. A community is a dynamic entity.

As mentioned in Chapter 1, Thomas Crombie Schelling's (2016) **focal points** are natural, special, or relevant solutions, references, intersections, interactions, connections, and integration points that people use in their interaction (OODA) with an experience (Cynefin) of reality (VUCA).

Individuals and collectives organize around focal points across an enterprise as well as anchor or bind together and un-anchor or un-bind from each other. The fluidity of individuals and flow of collectives determine the enterprise's antifragility.

We can achieve greater antifragility through:

- designing and creating an enterprise, which involves discovering an enterprise definition and establishing the enterprise
- evolving the enterprise and causing it to thrive, which involves enacting experience and embracing experiences.

Note, the activity of 'designing and creating' is perhaps a bit more separate than the activity of 'evolving and thriving'. But the activities of 'discovering' and 'establishing' the enterprise are not as separate or as linear as they may seem and the activities of 'enacting' and 'embracing' experiences are not as separate or as linear as they may seem.

Also note that any element of this approach may be used without going through the whole roadmap. So, if you are not ready for an end-to-end transformation journey, use any element to foster greater antifragility or use anything discussed in the previous chapters.

Ultimately, achieving greater antifragility requires architecting, designing, and creating as well as evolving and thriving using chaos or disruption – that is, 'chaos architecting' or 'disruption architecting'. And, rather than architect and scale fragility, as most enterprises do when they merely scale, achieving greater antifragility requires 'architecting for chaos' or 'architecting for disruption' or 'designing for chaos' or 'designing for disruption' to increase antifragility.

ENTERPRISE ANTIFRAGILITY

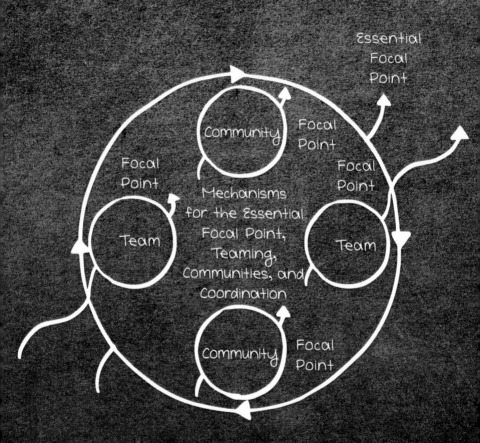

An antifragile enterprise is composed of a constellation of interconnected and flowing teams (via teaming) and a constellation of interconnected and flowing communities. These teams and communities both exist within a lattice alongside fluid individuals. Furthermore, multiple antifragile enterprises can form an antifragile ecosystem of antifragile enterprises where each enterprise has the characteristics of its individuals and collectives.

DESIGNING AND CREATING AN ENTERPRISE

Designing and creating an antifragile enterprise involves discovering a minimal enterprise definition and establishing the minimal enterprise.

While a traditional enterprise focuses on orchestrating organizational structures and coordinating processes to foster alignment, an antifragile enterprise focuses on a configuration and coordination that foster congruence and overall coherence. Notice that a traditional enterprise focuses on more long-lived structures and processes while an antifragile enterprise focuses on more long-lived communities, organized as communities of practice, and more short-lived teams, organized through teaming.

Furthermore, while a traditional enterprise focuses on integrating structures and processes into value streams, creating teams that contribute incremental value in a broad process of delivering value to clients and customers, an antifragile enterprise focuses on configurations and coordination to realize value. An antifragile enterprise is completely malleable, at all levels (individual, collective, and enterprise) and in every way. Too little structure and process will create chaos. Too much structure and process will dampen reality and aliveness and create inertia. At best, perhaps structure and process only offer guidance.

The **configuration** or business architecture of an antifragile enterprise is such that the individuals and collectives that constitute the enterprise, the aspects of the enterprise, can be re-woven into new configurations at any time. Individuals and collectives are strands that are woven and re-woven together into a tapestry, the fabric that is the enterprise. **Coordination** involves the individuals and collectives that constitute the antifragile enterprise integrating with one another around common focal points over time. **Congruence** involves the individuals and collectives that constitute the antifragile enterprise integrating with one another around common goals and common passions over time. **Coherence** involves the individuals and collectives that constitutive the antifragile enterprise forming a unified whole.

Discovering the Enterprise

Discovering, sometimes called discovering and defining, a minimal enterprise definition involves identifying individuals and collectives around dynamic focal points, which includes identifying individuals, teams, and communities as well as identifying mechanisms for teaming and organizing as communities.

Define the Enterprise

To discover a minimal enterprise definition, we must explore an enterprise's essential focal point. As human nature and every human endeavour can generally be explored as a meaningfully purposeful enterprise, an enterprise prospers if there is commitment to values and alignment on a cause – thus, a meaningfully purposeful enterprise within the context of an ecosystem.

- consider the enterprise's strategy, which is decomposed into results (solutions, experiences, products, and services)
- consider who is accountable for the strategy and for ensuring the enterprise prospers; an essential intention owner is commonly an executive who owns the portfolio of solutions, experiences, products, and services
- consider who is accountable for the actions concerning the strategy (all of the individuals, teams, and communities within the enterprise)
- consider who is accountable for the flow and pull concerning harmonization (all the individuals, teams, and communities within the enterprise that foster flow and pull within the enterprise).

Fundamentally, the essential focal point is the enterprise's main anchor and expresses the enterprise's identity. In many enterprises, the essential focal point is known as a strategy, vision, mission, or something similar, and it may be continuously re-imagined.

Define Teams and Communities

To define the enterprise's teams, explore the enterprise's goals, as discussed in Chapter 1.

- consider the enterprise's results and whom it serves
- consider who is accountable for the intentions concerning results (an intention owner)
- consider who is accountable for the actions concerning results (an action owner)

- consider who is accountable for flow and pull concerning harmonization (a dynamics owner).

Fundamentally, focal points are the enterprise's anchors through which it recognizes its clients and customers. In many enterprises, these focal points are known as products or services that constitute a products or services portfolio.

To define the enterprise's communities, explore people's passions. Fundamentally, focal points are the people's anchors through which the enterprise recognizes them. In many enterprises, these focal points are known as special-interest groups and include communities around portfolio management, service or product management, project management, technology architecture, or any other disciplines.

Define Mechanisms

To define a mechanism for working with an enterprise's essential focal point, explore how a group of individuals works with the enterprise's essential focal point. Fundamentally, any mechanism for working with the enterprise's essential focal point will relate to how the enterprise works with its strategy. In many enterprises, these mechanisms are played by a strategic leadership team and its sub-teams.

To define a mechanism for teaming, explore how a group of individuals may foster teams. Fundamentally, any mechanism for teaming will relate to how the enterprise works with teams, including launching, supporting, and disbanding teams. See the section on teaming in Chapter 3 for more information.

In many enterprises, these mechanisms are fulfilled by an 'office' team that manages services, products, portfolios, programs, or projects and its sub-teams.

To define a mechanism for organizing communities, explore how a group of individuals may foster communities. Fundamentally, any mechanism for organizing communities will relate to how the enterprise works with communities, including launching, supporting, and disbanding communities. See the section on communities in Chapter 3 for more information.

In many enterprises, these mechanisms are played by an 'office' team that manages portfolios, programs, and projects and its sub-teams.

To define a mechanism for coordination, explore any other focal points related to coordination (synchronization and cadence), spatially or temporally. Fundamentally, any mechanism for coordination will relate to how the teams, communities, and mechanisms will interact. In many enterprises, these mechanisms are fulfilled by a collection of calendars, ceremonies, or events.

Establishing the Enterprise

Establishing the minimal enterprise involves situating individuals and collectives around dynamic focal points, which includes situating individuals and launching teams and communities as well as launching the mechanisms for teaming and organizing as communities.

Launch Mechanisms

To launch a mechanism for working with an enterprise's essential focal point, establish a group that will work with the enterprise's essential focal point.

To launch a mechanism for teaming, establish a group of individuals who will foster teaming. Additionally, coordination considerations could include a team marketplace, fostered by the intention owners of the various teams within the enterprise, where teams could exchange team goals and all their related aspects, and teams could merge or split. To launch a mechanism for organizing communities, establish a group of individuals who will foster communities. Additionally, coordination considerations could include a community marketplace, fostered by the core groups of the various communities within the enterprise, where communities could exchange community subjects, including topics or subtopics, and all their related aspects, and communities could merge or split.

These mechanisms are teams organized around more foundational focal points, including a focal point and mechanism for working with an enterprise's essential focal point, a focal point and mechanism for teaming, and a focal point and mechanism for organizing communities.

To coordinate teams and communities, use a unified collection of focal points, related to coordination, spatially or temporally.

Launch Teams and Communities
To launch a team for each goal-based focal point, explore which specific individuals might be best suited to forming a performing team. Consider how individuals can form teams that can explore options and perform experiments based on their individual capabilities and competencies and how they can complement each other as a team.

Fundamentally, even if a team does not perform, individuals will reorganize through teaming. Exploring should involve as many individuals as possible, and individuals should then be invited to join teams; however, the invited individuals should retain the right to choose other teams. Identifying a single individual, an intention owner, to champion a focal point is a powerful way to empower individuals to galvanize other individuals as a team.

To launch a community for each passion-based focal point, explore which specific individuals might be best suited to being members of a community. Consider how individuals can form communities that can foster redundancy and distribute power based on their individual capabilities and competencies and how they can complement each other as a community.

Fundamentally, even if a community does not grow and mature, individuals will reorganize into other communities. Exploring should involve as many individuals as possible, and individuals should then be invited to join communities; however, the invited individuals should retain the right to choose other communities. Identifying a few individuals, a core group or 'nucleus', to champion a focal point is a powerful way to empower individuals to galvanize other individuals as a community.

EVOLVING AND THRIVING THROUGH EXPERIENCES

Evolving and thriving involves enacting experience and embracing experiences. Enacting experiences involves internal and external dynamics among individuals and collectives. Embracing experiences involves the enterprise internally evolving and externally thriving.

Enacting Experiences

Enacting, sometimes called developing and delivering, experiences involves internal and external dynamics among individuals and collectives, which includes individuals and collectives navigating and synchronizing with one another and signalling and triggering each other as they anchor or bind together and as they un-anchor or unbind from each other. An individual's fluidity across collectives and the enterprise is crucial. A collective's flow across the enterprise is crucial.

Scaffolding

Individual fluidity involves individuals navigating, synchronizing, signalling, triggering, anchoring and binding, and un-anchoring and unbinding. An individual is fluid across teams and communities relative to the essential focal point and other focal points.

Collective flow involves collectives navigating, synchronizing, signalling, triggering, anchoring and binding, and un-anchoring and unbinding. A team flows with other teams and a community flows with other communities relative to the essential focal point and other focal points.

Individuals and collectives are the scaffolding of the enterprise. Individuals and collectives are intertwined as their journeys and experiences unfold – through individual fluidity and collective flow – and as the enterprise adapts, survives, evolves, and thrives. Individuals and collectives are strands that are woven and re-woven together into a tapestry, the fabric that is the enterprise. Consider the following:

- **navigating** involves overall steering by observing and scanning, orienting, deciding and pivoting, and acting through our conversations, relationships, and behaviours in individual fluidity and collective flow around dynamic focal points that morph over time
- **synchronizing** involves intersecting, connecting, or coming together in individual fluidity and collective flow at dynamic focal points that morph over time
- **signalling** involves indicating or gesturing at events or moments to individuals or collectives as we are navigating and synchronizing
- **triggering** involves activating individual or collective dynamics at specific events or moments; these dynamics include conversing, relating, or behaving while we are navigating and synchronizing
- **anchoring or binding** together involves organizing around or connecting to dynamic focal points that morph over time as we are navigating and synchronizing and signalling and triggering
- **un-anchoring or unbinding** from each other involves un-organizing from or disconnecting from dynamic focal points that morph over time as we are navigating and synchronizing and signalling and triggering.

The words navigating, synchronizing, signalling, triggering, anchoring and binding, and un-anchoring and unbinding are used to distinguish the dynamics within an antifragile enterprise compared to those of a more traditional enterprise, where the enterprise is a system of structures and processes. Additionally, in an antifragile enterprise, teams, communities, and mechanisms must naturally and continuously morph over time as the enterprise adapts, survives, evolves, and thrives.

Micro-stressors

As a coach, I am a 'micro-stressor' or 'micro-disruptor' who creates micro-degrees of VUCA leveraging reality, the 'macro-stressor' or 'macro-disruptor', to:

- stress individuals, collectives, and enterprises relative to external forces in order for them to survive, thrive, and embrace reality
- stress individuals, collectives, and enterprises relative to internal forces in order for them to adapt, evolve, and ensure their aliveness.

Other micro-stressors (other than a formal coach) may be found in many enterprises.

Before coaching an enterprise, collective, or individual, we ensure that the enterprise, collective, or individual expresses authentic care about their clients and customers and intensions, exhibits sufficient openness to change, and is experiencing sufficient pain from its current conditions to consider changing.

A micro-stressor must be able to identify a specific source of stress and range of exposure that can be used to stress an individual, a collective, or an enterprise. A micro-stressor must also consider the variety and diversity of the sources of stress, the variety and diversity of the amount of stress, and the acuteness of the stress and necessary recovery time.

A micro-stressor must be able to activate the stress or provoke or nudge the individual, collective, or enterprise just enough to foster progress and not under-stress or over-stress the individual, collective, or enterprise:

- consider stress related to individuals, including their mindset, questions, leadership, conversations, relationships, and behaviours
- consider stress related to collectives, including their ability to work as a group, work with dysfunction, work with conflict, team through teaming, and organize as communities
- consider stress related to an individual, collective, or enterprise's adaptation and evolution
- consider stress related to an individual, collective, or enterprise's surviving and thriving.

A micro-stressor must be able to ensure that the individual, collective, or enterprise gains from the stress, helping the individual, collective, or enterprise to:

- create, discover, develop, and seize opportunities
- address threats and transform them into opportunities
- maximize and develop strengths
- minimize weaknesses and transform them into strengths
- adjust and develop its observations, orientation, decisions, and actions.

Antifragility Immune System

As micro-stressors stress (or micro-disruptors disrupt) individuals, collectives, and enterprises to encourage them to become more antifragile, individuals and collectives within the enterprises stress each other, which establishes the foundation of an emerging 'antifragility immune system'.

While an immune system serves to foster health by keeping out and destroying unhealthy things that may enter a body, an antifragility immune system serves to foster health by keeping extremely unhealthy or toxic things from entering a body, allowing reasonably unhealthy things with less toxicity to enter a body, destroying extremely unhealthy or toxic things that have entered a body, and allowing reasonably unhealthy things with less toxicity to stay in the body. This maintains a reasonable tension between healthiness and unhealthiness. Extremely unhealthy or toxic things cause death. Reasonably unhealthy things with less toxicity cause stress.

To ensure individual hygiene and health, collective hygiene and health, and overall enterprise hygiene and health so that the enterprise may adapt, survive, evolve, and thrive rather than die, the antifragility immune system fosters:

- the creation/launching and destruction/disbanding of teams and communities
- inviting or welcoming possibly valuable individuals into the enterprise
- uninviting or expelling possibly overly toxic individuals out of the enterprise but keeping reasonably unhealthy or less toxic individuals so as to foster internal stress
- rejecting possibly overly toxic individuals who want to enter the enterprise but inviting reasonably unhealthy or less toxic individuals so as to foster internal stress
- keeping possibly valuable individuals from exiting the enterprise.

Also, dynamics owners champion or facilitate the flow and pull between the intention owners and action owners, they champion the addressing of challenges that may impede or block that flow and pull between the intention owners and action owners, and they foster harmonization; thus, dynamics owners are commonly the nucleus for the antifragility immune system.

We must be cognizant that the antifragility immune system is not a kind of secret police but rather should emerge as a distributed function across the enterprise. And, again, excessive hygiene causes more fragility than antifragility.

Embracing Experiences
Embracing experiences involves an enterprise internally evolving and externally thriving, which involves embracing reality and ensuring aliveness.

Embracing Reality
Embracing reality involves having an empirical worldview and using heuristics regarding external dynamics among stakeholders and reality.

External dynamics among stakeholders involves stakeholders being entrepreneurs who experiment with options to confront disorder. Entrepreneurs are always exploring and seeking opportunities from which to thrive; as they encounter disorder and sufficiently and reasonably struggle, they consider their options and experiment, making small and reversible errors, which cause acute stress, distributed over time, with ample recovery time, to learn and grow.

Ensuring Aliveness

Ensuring aliveness involves having an essential world-view using heuristics regarding internal dynamics among stakeholders.

Internal dynamics among stakeholders involves stakeholders being adventurers who are small, non-specialized, and independent, and redundant with decentralized power. Adventurers are always exploring and seeking experiences from which to evolve. Individually, they don't specialize and are very independent; collectively, they don't compromise by specializing or becoming dependent, but become redundant and share power.

Antifragility Edge

Greater enterprise antifragility is only realized through greater individual antifragility and greater collective antifragility. The essence of antifragility is a delicate dance – at the antifragility edge – between embracing reality and ensuring aliveness, where disorder or stress is at the intersection.

We've explored this delicate dance between reality and aliveness throughout the book as well as how best to foster individual, collective, and enterprise antifragility.

Individual antifragility concerns our mindsets, questions, leadership, conversations, relationships, and behaviours. These exemplify our individual identity and our individual antifragility. This was explored in Chapter 2.

Collective antifragility concerns how we work as groups, work with dysfunction, work with conflict, team through teaming, and organize as communities. These exemplify our collective identity and our collective anti-fragility. This was explored in Chapter 3.

Enterprise antifragility concerns adapting, surviving, evolving, and thriving, both internally among individuals and collectives and externally within the context or environment of the enterprise. This was explored in Chapter 4.

Throughout the book, I have referenced many works that I have found to be demonstrably beneficial in fostering antifragility in practice, however there are other works that may be of value. We must be entrepreneurs and adventurers who are continuously and endlessly leveraging stress to discover other works for fostering antifragility.

Embodying an antifragility edge is perhaps best expressed by Taleb (2012):

Wind extinguishes a candle and energizes fire.

Likewise with randomness, uncertainty, chaos: you want to use them, not hide from them. You want to be the fire and wish for the wind.

Individually, collectively, and holistically, to embody an antifragility edge is to be fire.

REFERENCES

Adams, M G, 2016, *Change Your Questions, Change Your Life: 10 Powerful Tools for Life and Work*, Berrett-Koehler

Dweck, C, 2007, *Mindset: The New Psychology of Success*, Ballantine

Edmondson, A C, 2014, *Teaming: How Organizations Learn, Innovate, and Compete in the Knowledge Economy*, Jossey-Bass Pfeiffer

Glaser, J E, 2013, *Conversational Intelligence: How Great Leaders Build Trust and Get Extraordinary Results*, Routledge

Herrero, L, 2008, *Viral Change*, meetingminds

Holling, C S, 2001, *Panarchy: Understanding Transformations in Human and Natural Systems*, Island Press

International Coach Federation (ICF), viewed 2016, "Code of Ethics", http://coachfederation.org/about/ethics.aspx?ItemNumber=854

John Richard Boyd, viewed 2016, "John Boyd (military strategist)", http://en.wikipedia.org/wiki/John_Boyd_(military_strategist)

Lencioni, P, 2002, *The Five Dysfunctions of a Team: A Leadership Fable*, Jossey-Bass

Logan, D, King, J, Fischer-Wright, H, 2011, *Tribal Leadership: Leveraging Natural Groups to Build a Thriving Organization*, HarperBusiness

Schein, E, 2009, *The Corporate Culture Survival Guide*, Jossey-Bass

Schelling, T C, viewed 2016, "Thomas Schelling", http://en.wikipedia.org/wiki/Thomas_Schelling

Schumpeter, J A, viewed 2016, "Joseph Schumpeter", http://en.wikipedia.org/wiki/Joseph_Schumpeter

Snowden, D J, Boone, M E, 2007, "A Leader's Framework for Decision Making", Harvard Business Review, November

Taleb, N, 2012, *Antifragile: Things That Gain from Disorder*, Random House

Thomas, K W, Kilmann, R H, 2002, *Introduction to Conflict Management*, CPP

Tom Landry, viewed 2016, http://www.goodreads.com/quotes/58284-a-coach-is-someone-who-tells-you-what-you-don-t

Trautlein, B A, 2013, *Change Intelligence: Use the Power of CQ to Lead Change That Sticks*, Greenleaf Book Group Press

Tuckman, B W, 1965, "Developmental sequence in small groups", Psychological Bulletin, Volume 63, Number 6

U.S. Army War College, viewed 2016, "Volatility, uncertainty, complexity and ambiguity", http://en.wikipedia.org/wiki/Volatility,_uncertainty,_complexity_and_ambiguity

Wenger, É, 1999, *Communities of Practice: Learning, Meaning, and Identity*, Cambridge University Press

Wenger, É, 2014, *Learning in Landscapes of Practice: Boundaries, Identity, and Knowledgeability in Practice-based Learning*, Routledge

ABOUT
SINAN SI ALHIR

Si Alhir (Sinan Si Alhir) is an Entrepreneur, Author, Enterprise Business & Technology Transformation Coach, Trainer, Consultant, and Practitioner working with Individuals, Collectives/Communities/Teams, and Enterprises/Organizations.

He is a catalyst or alchemist with over four decades of proven experience in appreciating and leveraging all aspects of human dynamics to catalyze individuals, teams and communities, and whole enterprises to sustainably achieve impactful results towards meaningful intentions – bridging the chasm between strategy, leadership, and culture as well as business agility and antifragility through transformation/change-management. His clients have ranged from start-ups to the Fortune 500.

He is also affiliated with numerous prestigious professional organizations, holds various professional certifications, has authored various books, and contributes to and speaks at professional events.

Si can be reached at salhir@antifragilityedge.com.

Visit http://www.antifragilityedge.com for more.